COUNTER
DISCOURSE

-

IN AFRICAN LITERATURE

Smith and Ce [ed.]

AFRICAN

Library of Critical Writing

COUNTER DISCOURSE - in African Literature
Smith and Ce (Ed.)

©African Library of Critical Writing
Print Edition
ISBN: 978-9-7837-0856-3

For information address:
Progeny (Press) International
Email: progeny.int@gmail.com
For: African Books Network
9 Handel Str.
AI EBS Nigeria WA
Email: handelbook@gmail.com

Marketing and Distribution in the US, UK,
Europe, N. America (Canada),
and Commonwealth countries by

African Books Collective Ltd.
PO Box 721
Oxford OX1 9EN
United Kingdom
Email: orders@africanbookscollective.com

Contents

Introduction

FROM the discourse on black literary aesthetics using the prose and dramatic fictions of Anglophone, Lusophone and Francophone writers and her Diaspora, seven chapters emerge to give further prominence to counter inscriptions on Contemporary African literature. These are placed in three interactive phases of current critical discourses involving rejoinders from past to present and issues of cultural and contemporary modernity.

The first part tagged "Vocal Rejoinders" has the works of Nigeria's Femi Osofisan: *Tegonni: an African Antigone*, South Africa's JM Coetzee: *Foe*, and the South African novels of Neshani Andreas: *The Purple Violet of Oshaantu*, Bessie Head: *Maru*, and Yvonne Vera: *Under the Tongue* as probable models of the African writers' historic counter discourse be they "the jaundiced portrayal of Africa/Africans in Western canonical works" or "androcentric texts …(and) socio-cultural constructs."

Additional insights on other young writers of the African fictional tradition come in the second part aptly tagged "Contemporary Modernity." Here we investigate the relationship between literature and memory, and literature and political governance in Africa. These equally stress the argument that "African literature is hardly discussed outside contemporary history."

The dramas of Ama Ata Aidoo and Tess Onwueme are re-examined in the idea of "cultural translation" between African-American women in search of identity among their African counterparts. It is argued that "the reason for the lack of connection among groups in Africa and the Diaspora" can be traced to the unproven notion that "race … or –in the

Afrocentric scheme– a shared worldview, will automatically serve to draw disparate elements within the Diaspora to Africa" and advocates a "frank acknowledgement of difference" followed by the will to "understand the view of the other" and "renegotiate identity" as the structure for the widening of the frontier of African black heritage.

Writing on the semi-autobiographical novel of the Swiss-Gabonese writer, Bessora, we have noted how the diasporic Francophone author, with echoes of Senghor under colonial French rule, employs post-modernist surrealist imagery "to articulate a sense of unbelonging or anxiety-filled, hybrid state of the female immigrant in Paris."

Finally with the expose on ethno-lingual issues in South African (radio) drama as the concluding chapter, we have widened the (counter) discourse on Africa, embracing formerly uncharted currents in the imaginative literatures of the continent crystallizing in multi dimensional appreciation of her literary and cultural heritage.

-CS and CC

Vocal Rejoinders

Chapter One

Utter(ing) Silences

B.Weiss

[Culled from *Tangible Voice-Throwing: Empowering Corporeal Discourses in African Women's Writing of Southern Africa*. Bettina Weiss, Frankfurt: Peter Lang, 2004.]

WOMEN'S voice-throwing in Southern Africa is not a new phenomenon as such. It has always existed, but in varied intensities and restricted spheres. Sometimes !Kung women celebrated their womanhood with verve (Nisa: *The Life and Words of a !Kung Woman*, 2001); sometimes women subverted and ridiculed gender myths in oral storytelling. What is new, though, is that women have crossed the borderline of restricted spheres and have thrown their voices for everyone to hear.

Their voice is accusing and sexually daring as Jennifer's, the female protagonist in Dianne Case's *Toasted Penis and Cheese* (1999), who sarcastically dedicates her confessions to the perfect man "James Bond". Their voice is mocking as the one of a young Tswana woman's who, when repeatedly battered and abused by her husband, claims that she one day "got his finger and just chewed it" (*Stories of Courage* 51) or as Dorothy's, a prostitute in Virgina Phiri's collection of short stories entitled *Desperate* (2002), who takes revenge on her husband's lover by "chewing her ear until a piece of it came off in [...her] mouth" (31) and then triumphantly swallowing it, but not before displaying the piece in front of her humiliator and the community. Their voice is shocking as Nonceba's in Yvonne Vera's *The Stone Virgins* (2002), who describes her rape and her face being cut into pieces:

> [T]he moment is painless [...] then a piercing pain expands, [...] my body motionless [...]. He cut. Smoothly [..] quickly. Each part memorised [...]. My mouth a wound, [...] torn, pulled apart. A final cut, not slow, skilfully quick, the memory of it is the blood in my bones. (99)

And sometimes, women deliberately choose to refuse to throw their voice. They, in the true sense of the word, decide to be voiceless, yet as a means of subversion as depicted in Neshani Andreas's novel *The Purple Violet of Oshaantu* (2001) where Kauna defies convention by rejecting to speak at her husband's funeral. Not having a mouth –in this case deliberately– does not mean not to communicate because according to the basic law of communication: one cannot not communicate.[1] Every behaviour bears a message and Kauna's behaviour, for everyone to be registered, is very clear to a most shocking degree.

The following chapters deal with selected passages taken from novels written by Neshani Andreas, Bessie Head, and Yvonne Vera. They mark a departure from the mere notion that women react or write back, arguments that have often been overemphasised in literary criticism. In fact there is more to that: women act, that is to say, they take action, against their limited position by engaging in a discursive, dismantling, subverting, partly ironic, and deconstructing confrontation with androcentric texts not only of written material, but also, in a broader sense, of socio-cultural constructs and of texts written on the body. Reacting or writing back, in comparison, resembles a mimetic behaviour pattern,[2] too constricting and much less active than when taking action. Taking action refers to a woman's obligation to write down her own story, to enlarge the vision, and to unmake stereotyped allusions. She creates herself by exploring ambiguous multi-layered meanings which helps her to surpass the boundaries of agony and repression, to restore her mutilated body and mind –a prerequisite for authoring her selfhood.[3]

"Shades of Utter(ing) Silences" delves on the idea of women's potential to unveil constricting gender and racial laws by uttering silence, or as the title of the essay also suggests, by being enveloped in utter silence. This voicelessness, however, a cloister into the emotional space, is chosen deliberately and therefore distances itself from the mere notion of the Beti proverb of Cameroon: "Women have no mouth".

The printed dash or the empty page does not necessarily stand for absence and lack, but for gaps and blanks which set great store by what is left untold. The power of the uncommunicated lies in its speculation and interpretation. Silence is not always merely a helpless gesture or a capitulation, but can also be a resource as in Bessie Head's *Maru* (1971) or a reinforcement –in the sense of reinforcing a taboo, and thereby embodying the unspeakable, or a platform for finding a new voice as no "mouth can carry a sight such as that" (Vera *Nehanda* 23). To keep silent, to actively decide on being voiceless, as one encounters in *The Purple Violet of Oshaantu* (2001), may also be used as an instrument in order to subvert patriarchal traditions. As such, silence in all its facets and "as a will not to say or a will to unsay and as a language of its own has barely been explored" (Trinh 416).

In Southern African women's writing, silence can be traced as an option to overcome oppression, violation, and traumatic experiences. A case in point may be found in above mentioned novels and their protagonists: Kauna, an Owambo woman from the village Oshaantu in the northern part of Namibia, Margaret, a Masarwa woman from Dilepe in Botswana, and Zhizha, a young Shona girl from Zimbabwe. These women, though their cultural and geographical background are quite different, all have one thing in common: they suffer severely and in a moment of utmost distress they fall into utter silence.

Going Against Expected Voicing

In *The Purple Violet of Oshaantu*, (2001)[4] Kauna is degraded by her husband's frequent infidelity and battering. Her suffering is immense and she has all the reasons in the world to poison her husband, Shange, who one day drops dead in the living room of their house. Rumours spread that she had bewitched or poisoned him an accusation which proves to be untrue as it is later revealed he died of a heart attack. In the turmoil of death's revelation, Kauna goes mad for a couple of hours. She is hysterical and tries to convince everybody that her husband has just come home, did not touch his food, and that there was no evidence of her having bewitched or poisoned him.

The news that she had gone mad proved more sensational than the news of her husband's death. It is not Kauna herself who tells her story, but her best friend Ali. On the day of Shange's death, she is described as hysterical, with a dazed look in her eyes, and having the air of the village's mentally disturbed women (PV 11-12). After the first day, as Ali observes, she sleeps intensely, is uninterested in the preparation of the funeral, and does not shed a tear –sadness is totally lacking. Her behaviour is indifferent, partly mocking, partly good-humoured, but it is also considered as estranging, insulting, and outrageous by family and community.

11

The oshiWambo proverb "a woman is the house," which stands for the notion that the wife is the closest person to her husband (PV 100), is applied by Shange's relatives to force Kauna to confess where her husband's wealth is safely kept. Kauna refuses to designate someone to give a speech on behalf of the widow on the day of the funeral (PV 137-140). The speech on behalf of the widow is given by a person who is very close to the widow and who will say some favourable words about the deceased. The words, however, have either been told to the speaker or written down by the widow herself and must reflect her personal sentiments. This is the custom and to disregard this tradition is taboo. Kauna disobeys this custom by applying a behaviour pattern which is normally favoured by the patriarchal society – a woman's silence.

The church service program lists all the 'on behalf' speeches followed by the speaker's name. The 'on behalf of the widow' speech only shows a blank space which tells a lot by what is left untold (PV 158). Suppressed excitement is in the air when the woman in charge of the funeral program repeatedly calls for a voluntary speaker. Nobody moves, Ali is perspiring heavily, and Kauna is described as "[n]ot giving a damn in the least" (PV 159).

By exporting the law of women's silence into a realm of publicly expected voicing, Kauna beats patriarchy with its own weapons. This outrage is sketched rather grotesquely in the appearance of Kuku Peetu, her favourite uncle. He spontaneously decides to hold the speech. It is less his words, but rather his clothes, described as "navy-blue wrinkled blazer, pink shirt and yellow pants [... and] a lime-green handkerchief [...]" (PV 159-160), which contrast with the mourning scene. He looks like a parrot parodying the expected words on behalf of the widow. Though this is not a victory for the fact of not having given a speech on behalf of the widow, it is a moral victory for Kauna as she could carry through her will of uttering silence and hence making the unspeakable visible: her year-long disgrace and oppression.

Deep Pool of Creativity and Power

The late African-American Audre Lorde once described women's inner silent spaces as "the home of great potential":

> Silence [...] is a site not only of resistance but of transformation, the home from which new dreams and visions are born. [... S]ilences [.. are] deep pools where "each one of us holds an incredible reserve of creativity and power, of unexamined and unrecorded emotion and feeling." (qtd. in Stone 20)

In *Maru* (1971), Margaret Cadmore is such a woman. She is an orphan who is categorised by the derogative term Masarwa or Bushman and is treated like an outcast. Her namesake and foster mother Margaret Cadmore brings her up with love and dignity, which does not, however, shield her from society's vicious racial stereotyping. In Botswana, Masarwa people are considered "untouchable[s] to the local people [...]" (13) and the remote village Dilepe is a stronghold of the most powerful chiefs where Masarwa are held as slaves.

As a teacher at Leseding in Dilepe, Margaret passes as Coloured, but she insists on enlightening people about her true identity. She tells everyone that she is a Masarwa and as a consequence faces severe mobbing and hostility. She is threatened with dismissal from school and suffers from loneliness. Her suffering is intensified by her unfulfilled love for Moleka, a Tswana and a son of a tribal chief, and, as Margaret sees it, by the indifference of Maru, the eldest Tswana son of a paramount chief and Moleka's best friend.

Besides school and the hours spent with Maru's sister, Dikeledi, Margaret is surrounded by an inner quietness when she is by herself:

> Her own heart was so peaceful. She stood where she was, empty-handed, but something down there belonged to her in a way that triumphed over all barriers [...]. It was continuous, like the endless stretch of earth and sky, [...] as though her heart said: 'Wait and that will grow in its own time. Wait and you will grow in your own time, but slowly, like eternity.' [...] [S]he sat down and stared deep into her own, peaceful heart. (99)

The house where Margaret is staying is an abandoned old library –books are missing. The metaphorical lack of letters is a suitable environment where Margaret in her solitude and silence finds a source for her creativity and power. She has visions and dreams which she expresses in drawings. Her dear friend Dikeledi supplies her with crayons, oils, drawing ink, water colours, paper, and brushes and orders Margaret to, as she calls it, "experiment with everything" (100) she has brought along. Margaret's state of quietness, which one may regard as a well of inner peacefulness, now experiences a new rhythm which is slowly increasing into days and nights of feverish painting.

On her quest Margaret discovers her unexamined and unrecorded emotions about which Audre Lorde spoke. Her body becomes a "power machine of production" (101) which she cannot control. These emotions, visions, and dreams are not expressed by words, but by decisive and powerful strokes mediated through crayons, water colours, and oils. Three of these drawings form a mosaic: a house in the dark with bright windows; heavy, dark clouds hanging in the sky are contrasted by a field of bright-yellow daisies; and a path running along the field of daisies with a black couple embracing at the end of this path, one of which Dikeledi identifies as Maru (103-104). Maru, whose name stands for the seTswana word "the elements" (Vigne 104), proves to be the sole supporter of Margaret's visions; he calls himself a dreamer, he has thedreams as Margaret, and he is creative in his ideas –a trait normally assigned to women and less to men. He is the one who makes his dreams come true. It is Margaret's foster mother visionary same who professed to Margaret in her early childhood that she will help her people one day, and it is the three drawings which anticipate Margaret's vision and dreams of transcending the racial discrimination between the Tswana and Masarwa people. Silence not only resided in Margaret, but also dominated Maru's and Margaret's relationship, and only Margaret's paintings mediated their bond which brought "the wind of freedom" to the Masarwa and "some kind of strange, sweet music you could hear over and over again" to Margaret (*Maru* 124, 127).

Platform for a New Language

Silence and giving voice in *Under the Tongue* (1996)[5] has been mainly considered under the aspect of "the role of language as a medium of healing from trauma" (Samuelson, "Grandmother Says" 2) or the necessity of breaking silence.[6] The following section will focus on the role of silence as a necessary platform for finding a new language which, as it is argued, gives silence an enlarged, productive dimension.

In reading Yvonne Vera's *Under the Tongue* one is reminded of what Lisa F. Signori calls, in reference to the French author Marguerite Duras, a livre brûlé. The story of Duras's experimental novel *La pluie d'été* (1990) presents an image of a livre brûlé which has a burned hole in the middle making the text of the book unreadable. The words are destroyed, similar to Zoë Wicomb's *David's Story* (2000) where the letters of David's story flow out of the computer due to a bullet which has destroyed the monitor. The notion that the present, dominant language can satisfactorily narrate all experience is subverted by these incidents. As suggested by Signori, "meaning must be inferred from the remaining, charred words that surround the hole, and must ultimately be recovered in the blank, in the hole left behind" (121). What serves for Duras is also applicable in a figurative sense for Vera's Under the Tongue: language is pushed "to the limit and delves into the silence at the heart of language, into the hole, the vide out of which a new beginning is possible" (Signori 121).

By listening to her inner monologue, a speaking from within the body, one follows Zhiza's story of repeated raping by her father, while her mother Runyararo was among the women who had fought beside men during the war. The story of *Under the Tongue* begins and ends with the incestuous rape act which gives the story a cyclical structure, a structure which might hint at the recurring drama of rape in the microcosm of the family and, in a metaphorical sense, in the macrocosm of society where the exploitation of a woman's body is closely linked to the conquering and exploitation of land.[7]

The taboo of incestuous rape resides in Zhiza's mouth, buried like a stone under her tongue. Zhiza's mother, Runyararo, her name stands emblematic for "quietness" (Eppel 13), loses no words, when she comes to know of her husband's rape act. She kills him –the unspeakable is made public in an unspoken performance, in an act of murder and her subsequent imprisonment. She remains silent as the act of rape is too horrible to speak of, and can only be answered by another taboo: a wife killing her husband. When Runyararo is confronted by her mother after having killed her husband, the

16

words of anger and bewilderment lay astray on the floor, unsuitable to name what has to be named. The scattered words are futile and leave both women in "[t]heir waiting [which] is silent with no words to accompany it" (UT 32).

It can be suggested that for Zhizha incestuous rape is more than an "unsayable word" (6) as Stephen Gray puts it. It is an unspeakable word, a taboo, which she keeps under her tongue.[8] Zhiza remains silent, but not as a means to retreat as a victim, but as a Signorian delving into silence, into the hole, the vide out of which a new beginning is possible. She is anxious to

> listen to Grandmother, to discover her places of silence. [... She knows that] there is a wide lake in her memory, a lake in which ripples grow to the edges of the sky, a lake in which all our grief is hidden [where grandmother's ..] word rests at the bottom of silent lakes, (70)

the word which will ultimately be given to her. In one of her tormented nights one learns that she "listen[s] to the softness in the silence [... and] remember[s] [.. her] scar" (21). Nightmares and her fragmentary inner monologue replace her outward silence. The traumatic rape experience leads to the loss of language. Her voice, as she puts it, is "pulled from its roots [...], empty and forgotten" (3).

The voice, it can be argued, is forced to die and it is necessary to plunge into silence, and –to borrow Signori's words– into "the hole, the vide" (121) as there is no place to speak about this horrific tale, as there is "no mouth left" (86) as Mazvita, the protagonist of another of Vera's novels entitled *Without a Name*, (1994) determines. Though, Zhizha is aware that her "tongue is a river," but for the time being it "is heavy with sleep" (UT 1, emphasis added). The tongue, in order to speak, has to be a river, it has to be filled with water like a

17

riverbed after heavy rains. Pulling at the root, the origins, as grandmother does, is closely connected with water: river, lake, rain, and tears. There is a link to the Shona mythology of lakes and rivers being the source of life (Baumann 221), and it is grandmother who is said to be a river, whose body harbours the river. She is said to be the source of life who has "placed it there before [Zhizha] was born, before [Zhizha's] mother was born" (UT 1). Yet, the river remains in a silent waiting, to be remembered, for Zhizha will only find the source of life/being, that is, she will only heal, if she does allow herself to go into the river, or, as she puts it, to be "inside Grandmother," "[... to be] Grandmother" (2).

Enveloped in this silence, one witnesses Zhizha's gradual "awakening" (1). Only a murmur, coming from her grandmother and observed through quiet body movements, Zhizha sees her grandmother's "eyes pull this root from inside her [...] her lips tremble, her arms so silent, her voice departed, her elbows bare [...] she waits [...]" (1-2).

Zhizha acknowledges her knowing that grandmother's "waiting is also her giving" (1-2). They all wait: Zhizha, her grandmother, and Runyararo, her mother. Grandmother waits for her voice to find "the forgotten, the departed, who wait[s] to be remembered" and Runyararo and Zhiza wait for the healing of grandmother's voice-throwing to the moon when darkness falls (9, 11).[9] They all wait for the same: finding a new language to speak the unspeakable; and all this waiting holds an element of tense quietness. Being confronted with the unspeakable and trying to find a new language to unveil the taboo also breaks open old scars. A nightmare perpetuates another nightmare and Zhizha fearfully waits for the horrifying sound indicating grandmother's death (UT 12).[10] She describes her body parts as dissolving, enlarging, and as discovering "their own ability for silence" (12-13).

It may be argued that she could most probably not overcome her emotional scarring on her own as the parent-child relationship is a significant factor in a child's traumatic experience. In addition, in therapeutic intervention the mother as a co-therapist plays a significant role in mastering the trauma (Leibowitz et al. 104, 106-107). In fact, Zhizha's healing is possible with the help of her mother in form of flashback fantasies which emerge into a dreamlike awakening (UT 80-82, 95, 97). The play between mother and child of repeating, reading, and writing the syllables "a e i o u" initiate a new phase of life, a new beginning which Zhizha replays in front of the mirror:

> I watch myself through the mirror, [...] till tears fall down my cheeks. [...] I sit up straight like my mother [...] and sternly say repeat after me a e i o u, then I change into me, and I say a e i o u. [...] I have turned into mother, and she laughs, because she has become me. (81-82)

The presence of the mother, though, is not real, but is constituted by Zhiza's intermingled fantasies, flashbacks, and dreams. Grandmother's words calming her down: "sh sh sh you only have a fever you will soon be well" (95) and Zhizha's wishful longing: "I wish my mother would stay, but I meet her in dream" (97) refer to these phantasmic encounters.

It is quite obvious that Zhiza's mother is sentenced for life and will not return home as women's offences are treated differently before the court than men's. As one is told in the short stories of Bessie Head, in contrast to a man who is only sentenced for a few years for killing his wife which is considered as "a crime of passion" or, in the worst case, as a "mess and foolishness" ("Life" 46), a woman who kills her husband will be sentenced to life imprisonment as she has been charged with "Man-slaughter" ("Collector" 88).

Zhizha's healing is also, and especially, possible with the help of her grandmother who takes the place of her absent mother. Interestingly, the grandmother has no name –a suggestion that she may be an epitome of the Grand-Mother of maternal voice, a voice or a new language which Meg Samuelson justifiably asserts as "feminising culture as the opposition between nature (mother) and culture (language) is broken down [...]. Language is returned to the realm of the body" ("Grandmother" 30-31). Yet, it is also Zhizha who plays a major part in overpowering the horror: In the act of naming, Zhizha is her mother and her mother is Zhizha's grandmother (UT 14-15).

The cyclical corporeality displays the mutually endured pains and the travelling through these "territories of pain" (Veit-Wild 346) results in a re-membering which leaves the grandmother with empty eyes and arms, an emptiness which is a burden too heavy to carry. This emptiness, this silence has to be filled with new dreams, and new dreams are only possible if the unspeakable is aired. To air the unspeakable, in turn, necessitates a new language.[11] Zhizha sets great effort in helping grandmother to find this new language by metaphorically placing a basket which is waiting as it is being described "with words to be shelled and tossed, waiting with words to be chosen, cast aside, separated, dismissed" into grandmother's arms:

> I [Zhizha] look at the basket and know that the best words are those that are shared and embraced, those that give birth to other words more fruitful than themselves, stronger than themselves. [...] I move my feet toward the tarnished wall and reach for the basket. The basket is far above my head but the rope is nearer so I pull hard at the rope which holds the basket to the wall and the basket falls

into my waiting arms. There is a basket in my arms. I carry the basket across the silent room. I notice that my feet are my feet and I have also found my arms. I give the basket to Grandmother. I place it safely under her embrace. She touches my arms with hopeful caress.

She moves her right hand inside the basket to gather something she has recently discovered, something that she has lost while gathering words. (16)

Zhizha needs her grandmother just as she needs her mother, and her mother needs her and grandmother just as grandmother needs Zhizha and Runyararo. This symbiotic support is where women come together, where they re-member, where their tears form a river, and where the river forms a tongue where voices hide and where, as Zhiza observes, a "healing silence" presides; it is in silence, she asserts, a dream will germinate, grow, and will not be lost (41).

In fact, this reading of Under the Tongue carefully suggests that there are two types of silence: the one which paralyses and the one which helps to re-member, to heal. It is a silence which offers a platform for a new language which starts with "the word" that grandmother has given to Zhizha and which she has to recollect.[12] The maternal voice gives the word to a woman who gives it back or hands it over to another. The word is "a place where women harvest" (54).

Throwing voicelessness is, as the above examples have shown, a further means to go against oppression, exploitation, and distress. It serves the women as an instrument to rebel against patriarchal conventions, to find the necessary power to go against racist practices, and to find a new language to overcome traumatic experience of male induced violence. This essay is especially interesting as silence has, to the best of my knowledge, only been regarded in the context of silencing women or women falling into silence as passive victims. *The Purple Violet of Oshaantu, Maru,* and *Under the Tongue* impressively depict that silence can be read in a quite different and liberating way.

Chapter Two

Reworking the Canon

A.Kehinde

Africa in Western Canons

A CENTURY of European (British and French mainly, but also Portuguese, German, Italian and Spanish) colonization left behind an African continent dazed, bewildered and confused. This is why modern African writers see the need for and admit a commitment to the restoration of African values. In fact, the Western world equates knowledge, modernity, modernization, civilization, progress and development to itself, while it views the Third-World from the perspective of the antithesis of the positive qualities ascribed to itself.[1] Such negative stereotypes are perpetrated by a system of education, which encourages all the errors and falsehoods about Africa/Africans. Writing on the jaundiced portrayal of Africa/Africans in Western canonical works, Edward Wilmot Blyden asserted over a hundred years ago that:

> All our traditions and experiences are connected with a foreign race –we have no poetry but that of our taskmasters. The songs which live in our ears and are often on our lips are the songs we heard sung by those who shouted while we groaned and lamented. They sang of their history, which was the history of our degradation. They recited their triumphs, which contained the records of our humiliation. To our great misfortune, we learned their prejudices and their passions, and thought we had their aspirations and their power. (91)

Africa and Africans are given negative images in Western books of geography, travels, novels, history and in Hollywood films about the continent. In these texts and records, Africans are misrepresented; they are portrayed as caricatures. Unfortunately, Africans themselves are obliged to study such pernicious teachings. Reacting to this mistake, Chinua Achebe declares that if he were God, he would "regard as the very worst our acceptance, for whatever reason, of racial inferiority" (32). He further comments that his role as a writer is that of an educator who seeks to help his society regain belief in itself and put away the complexes of the years of vilification and self-denigration.

Homi Bhabha also declares that Western newspapers and quasi-scientific works are replete with a wide range of stereotypes (17). In similar fashion, Andrew Milner and Jeff Browitt dwell on the inscriptions of stereotypes of Africa/Africans in Western religious canonical texts (the Bible in particular). To them, canonical texts are:

> those Christian religious texts considered divinely inspired by the Church. In secular aesthetics, literary and other texts accorded a privileged status, within some version or another of a 'great tradition', as embodying the core values of a culture. (225)

Thus, in expansion of Milner and Browitt, Dennis Walder asserts that the Western-associated canons of texts are dotted with a whole complex of conservative, authoritarian attitudes, which supposedly buttress the liberal-democratic (bourgeois) states of Europe and North Africa (74). Actually, the colonization of Africa is explicit in the physical domination and control of its vast geographical territory by the colonial world and its cronies. However, this physical presence, domination and control of Africa by the colonizer is sustained by a series or range of concepts implicitly constructed in the minds of the colonized. Therefore, more than the power of the cannon, it is canonical knowledge that establishes the power of the colonizer "I" over the colonized "Other" (Foucault 174). It should also be stressed that the available records of Africa's history handed down by the Europeans, far from being a disinterested account of Africa, are interested constructs of European representational narratives. This view is supported by Ania Loomba : "the vast new world (Africa inclusive) encountered by European travelers were interpreted by them through ideological filters, or ways of seeing, provided by their own culture" (71).

The English novel is the "terra firma" where the self-consolidating project of the West is launched, and Robinson Crusoe is an inaugural text in the English novel tradition. It is also an early eighteenth-century testament to the superiority of rational civilization over nature and savagery, a text that foregrounds the developing British Empire's self-representation through encounters with its colonial Others. Crusoe, the eponymous hero of the novel, anticipates the Hegelian Master. A postcolonial reading of the novel, however, reveals that Defoe discloses –however unwittingly– some deeper ideological operations: Western colonialism is not content with pillaging human and material resources to sustain and consolidate its power over its colonies; it has to destroy the indigenous cultures and values (religion, language, dressing codes, etc) and supplant them with distorted and totally ambivalent versions. As Frantz Fanon asserts:

> Colonialism is not satisfied merely with holding a people in its grip and emptying the native's brain of all form and content. By a kind perverted logic, it turns to the past of the oppressed people, and

distorts, disfigures and destroys it. This work of devaluing pre-colonial history takes on a dialectical significance today. (168)

By distorting the history and culture of Africa, the colonizer has created a new set of values for the African. Consequently, just the subject fashioned by Orientalism, the African has equally become a creation by the West. On his 'island', Crusoe attempts to subjugate all of nature, including Friday, his manservant. The founding principle of subjugation is force, as he uses his gun to save Friday from his captors (and to silently threaten Friday into obedience). He then begins a programme of imposing cultural imperialism.

The first method in this programme is a linguistic one. Crusoe gives Friday his new name without bothering to enquire about his real name. He instructs Friday to call him "Master." He thus initiates Friday into the rites of English with a view to making him just an incipient bilingual subject. He teaches him just the aspects of the English language needed for the master-servant relationship –to make Friday useful, handy and dependent. The master-servant orders suggest how Africans and other 'natives' have been tabulated and classified by the West throughout colonial (and neocolonial) history. The second method is theological.' Crusoe's attitude to Friday's religion is akin to the later imperialist missionaries' attitude to the indigenous religions they encountered on African soil. Crusoe sees African traditional religion as blindly ignorant pagan creed. He believes that his own (Western) God is the true God, and that he is doing Friday an invaluable service by converting him. As constructed moral and cultural inferiors, then, indigenous people are 'naturally' suited to work for Westerners; when Crusoe wants to build a boat, for instance, he assigns Friday and his father the dirty and difficult tasks, while the Spaniard is merely to supervise. Perhaps to justify such incipient tyranny, Crusoe sees all natives as savages (marked most of all by their cannibalism) and constantly refers to them as such:

> All my apprehensions were buried in the thoughts of such a pitch of inhuman, hellish brutality, and the horror of the degeneracy of human nature, which though I had heard of often, yet I never had so near a view of before; in short, I turned away my face from the horrid spectacle. (163)

With tongue, pen, gun and Bible, Crusoe is able to prove and assert his superiority and assume a new mantle of power. He is a 'Master' who controls and thus can exploit his environment, a budding imperialist conveniently furnished with an inferior Other to reflect, even constitute, the superior Self. James Joyce also identifies some prototypes of colonial experience in *Robinson Crusoe* in forms of colonization, subjugation, exploitation and Christianization of the colonized:

> The true symbol of the British conquest is Robinson Crusoe, who cast away on a desert island, in his pocket a knife and a pipe, becomes an architect, a carpenter, a knife grinder, an astronomer, a baker, a shipwright, a potter, a saddler, a farmer, a tailor, an umbrella maker and a clergyman. He is the true prototype of the British colonist, as Friday (the trusty savage who arrives on an unlucky day) is the symbol of the subject races. (qtd. in Gallagher 170)

Throughout *Robinson Crusoe*, the protagonist embodies Western mercantile capitalism, grounded in a colonial economy, through his money-making schemes (engaging in the slave trade, investing profits, hoarding gold on the island) and his moral lapses (most notably, selling the Moorish boy with whom he escaped from the Turkish pirates for sixty pieces of silver). On the other hand, the natives, represented by

Friday, are depicted as careless self-indulgent individuals who lack forethought or reflections. This is why the white man who has a life of reason, introspection and faith, intervenes, like the Almighty God, to civilize the savage Other.

Although Friday is described specifically as not black, and as possessing non-Negroid features, he represents the Black Africans in *Robinson Crusoe* even more than he represents Amerindians (which he presumably is). The novel is set on a New World island; British colonialism at that time was centered in the Caribbean and its slave-based plantation economy. As most native Caribs, Arawaks and Tainos had been annihilated through war and disease, slaves were supplied from Africa. The triangular trade itself blurred spatial boundaries and, by importing a new 'native Other' to replace the old 'native Other,' blurred ethnic distinctions as well. Every one who is not white becomes 'black.' It is precisely this developing Manichean dichotomy, a direct consequence of the myth of civilization based on repression, that Robinson Crusoe records.

In Defoe's *Robinson Crusoe*, Crusoe the Western European self is equated with futurity, vision, civilization, rationality, language and light. Conversely, the depiction of the non-European (the Amerindians, the African) in the text is an absolute negation of the Other. The black is associated with pre-history, savagery, cannibalism, unconsciousness, silence and darkness. Crusoe, the archetypal Western man, assumes the posture of a king, a prince, a governor, a general, and a field marshal. He is worried by the sense of his self-assumed greatness. He suffers the pang of delusions of grandeur, seeing himself as some kind of God. This temper is reflected in his unconscious (his dreams) most especially, in which he rescues a savage from his enemies. The so-called savage kneels down to Crusoe as a sign of reverence, praying him for assistance.

To a great extent, Crusoe has the passion of racial consciousness. In fact, he is "an unlikable man for [a] hero" (Palmer 10), an egoist who has little interest in anyone but himself. In his portrayal of Africa/Africans/Amerindians, Defoe was expressing an opinion common to his contemporaries. *Robinson Crusoe* articulates the European attitude about the peoples of Africa and America that structured an expanding imperialist venture. Once considered a model for alternative Rousseauean concepts of education and growing up, the 'Robinsonade' and its protagonist (Crusoe) have had to face harsh criticism. In fact, Crusoe, his kith and kin, and Defoe, the author, are guilty of ethnocentrism, logocentrism, proto-imperialism, and even megalomania. Crusoe is not a role model in this multicultural, pluralistic world of ours. Instead, he plays a role that begs to be rewritten –thus the existence of alternative versions of the Robinson myth in post-colonial fiction, including Coetzee's *Foe*.

Countering Misrepresentation: Post-Colonial Literature in Dialogue with Western Canonical Works

What is today known as colonial discourse, post-colonial theory or postcolonialism is an offshoot of the anti-colonial activism and writings of such nationalists as Leopold Sedar Senghor, Frantz Fanon and Amilcar Cabral (Bill, et al 63; Schipper 82; Zukogi 17). The early writings of the nationalists set the tone, pace and character of the debate in the field today. The publication of four key texts whose views many Africans largely share also energized the tempo of counter-discourse in Africa. These texts are Fanon's *The Wretched of the Earth* (originally published posthumously in 1961); Walter Rodney's *How Europe Underdeveloped Africa* (1972); Said's *Orientalism* (originally published in 1978); and Chinweizu, et al's *Toward the Decolonization of African Literature* (1980). These counter-hegemonic texts decentered, even undermined the intellectual heritage of the Western Academy while questioning the foundational assumptions behind the Western colonial/ imperial/neocolonial project.

Similarly, African writers (for example, Achebe, Ngugi, Salih, Armah, Kane) critique European imperialism. The fact that a significant portion of contemporary African literature is preoccupied with reworking Western canonical works is a logical and natural –rather than a misplaced and belated– response. This is because Africa's contact with Europe has impacted greatly on its socio-cultural, political, economic and psychological well-being. The 'dislocation', psychic and physical debilitation that this contact has created, is so enormous that it rarely escapes the critical attention of African writers, and more recently, of the post-colonial discourse analyst. As Ime Ikiddeh claims in his Foreword to Ngugi's *Homecoming*:

> There can be no end to the discussion of African encounter with Europe because the wounds inflicted touched the very springs of life and have remained unhealed because they are constantly being gashed open again with more subtle, more lethal weapon. (xii)

African literature's fundamental engagement is with the colonial presence in Africa, dismantling its dehumanizing assumptions and resisting its pernicious consequences. The African novel, in particular, reflects an evolving consciousness at once historical, cultural, and political. It strives to counter the negative picture of Africa and Africans promulgated by some European writers, including Joyce Cary, Graham Greene, Joseph Conrad, Ryder Haggard, Daniel Defoe, William Shakespeare and the like. Even as African novelists seek to interrogate and modify European racism and exploitation[2] in literature as well as in practice, they use their writings to 'bridge' the cultural gap between 'Blacks' and 'Whites.' Their reactions to precursor colonial canonical works emphasize their own difference and unique qualities. They claim their own culture, aesthetics, history and essence. This nationalist temper is also reflected in many movements (like PanAfricanism, the Black Renaissance, Negritude, Black Consciousness) that search for African roots and black traditions. In Schipper 's words:

> The medium of the novel proved very suitable to the needs of African writers who wanted to address colonial reality as they have experienced it. In their work, the novelists uprooted the myth that riches and power make the white man superior (37-38).

African writers see the need to tell their people's and continent's stories themselves. According to Ernest Emenyonu, any attempt to relinquish this God-given right would "allow foolish foresters stray in and mistake the middle of a mighty African baobab for an African tree trunk"(4). The idea that only one group of privileged people (in this case, Europeans) is qualified to interpret the world should be interrogated. For instance, Achebe, in *Things Fall Apart* (1958) and his other polemical writings, claims that the missionaries and explorers have lied about Africa. He argues that the depictions of the human and political landscapes of Africa enshrined in Western canonical works are biased and ignorant. Achebe thereby assumes the task of retelling the African stories and asserting the primacy of African culture. To Achebe, the ultimate service of African writers to their people is to make African society regain belief in itself and put away the complexities of years of denigration and self-abasement (165).

Inheriting Achebe's legacy, contemporary African critics and writers are required to act with integrity and dedication. This is because the colonial discourses about Africa/Africans need to be subjected to further reworking with a view to correcting erroneous notions about Africa and her peoples. In the words of Walder (4), "these works require a new sense of their place in the changing world of today, if they are to retain their freshness and relevance" (4). Whether these reworkings take the form of 'national allegories', as Fredric Jameson (85) suggests, or appear as inversions of black/white or center/periphery binaries or question binary structures of thought themselves3 they must keep responding not only to the burdens of the past but also to the exigencies of the present and the challenges of the future.

Salman Rushdie, in his much quoted statement "The Empire writes back with a vengeance" to the imperial "centre", admits that postcolonial writing is imbued with nationalist assertion which involves the "Other" claiming itself as central and self-determining, by questioning the basis of European and British metaphysics (336). The postcolonial writers therefore challenge the world-view that can polarize centre and periphery in the first place. On his part, Fanon sees the dichotomy (colonizer/ colonized) as a product of a 'manichaeism delirium', the result of which condition is a radical division into paired oppositions such as good-evil, true-false, and white-black (81). This dichotomy is absolutely privileged in the discourse of the colonial relationship. Thus, the colonial discourse needs new liberating narratives to free the colonized from this disabling position. Therefore, the central 'postcolonialist' argument is that "postcolonial culture has entailed a revolt of the margin against the metropolis, the periphery against the centre, in which experience has become 'uncentred', pluralistic and nefarious" (Ashcroft, et al 12).

In his "Representing the Colonized", Said prioritizes narratives which take the Third-World seriously by placing what it has to say on equal terms with its own explanations ("Representing" 206). Also, Gayatri Spivak is highly critical of the current intellectual enterprise of constituting the colonial subject as Other in her "Can the Subaltern Speak?" (68). No place is created for the subaltern (raced) to speak, as colonialism's narrativization of African culture effaces all traces of black's voice. She believes that postcolonial critics should concentrate on articulating the margins and gaining control of the way in which the marginalized are represented; the postcolonial intellectual should also break with the paradigms of representation that promote antagonism between the First and Third Worlds.

J.M. Coetzee's Foe *and the Debunking of Racial and Patriarchal Egoism in Defoe's* Robinson Crusoe

Chinua Achebe, J.M. Coetzee, Wilson Harris, George Lamming, Patrick White, Margaret Atwood, Jean Rhys and other postcolonial writers have rewritten particular works from the English canon "with a view to restructuring European 'realities' in postcolonial terms, not simply by reversing the hierarchical order, but by interrogating the philosophical assumptions on which that order was based" (Ashcroft 33). The African story continues to be (re)told by postcolonial writers. When Coetzee's *Foe* was published in 1986, it added to the growing corpus of counter-discursive writings in postcolonial literature. Although Coetzee is among the most critically revered of world writers, he is also one of the most misunderstood and misrepresented African writers. At least, this is the opinion of critics like Kwaku Korang and Andre Viola, who observe that a problem in Coetzee's fiction is the difficulty of reconciling a liberal humanist approach with the reality of the oppressive power hegemonies in South Africa, which negate such a vision. However, a careful consideration of the various systems of oppression with which Coetzee's novels contend provides a powerful antidote to viewing him as an 'apolitical' relativist. The critic of Coetzee's fiction should be less concerned with the fiction's absolute or historical truth than with its fictional truth as embodied in the narrative. His works engage with a vast literary heritage and question authority is invested in literary discourse, as well as investigate power dynamics and political oppression and ethical responsibility.

Foe takes up some central postcolonial issues, which include the following: who will write? (that is, who takes up the position of power, pen, in hand?); who will remain silent? (the issues of silencing and speech); how do colonial regimes distribute and exercise power? (and, in consequence, create zones of powerlessness). Attempting to demythologize a dominant knowledge about empire, Foe is imbued with a 'fresh' paradigm; its textual universe is tailored towards not only revisiting but also retracting the long line of epistemic violence foisted on the psyche and intellect of the Other. The text seeks to uncover the silence and oppression at the heart of Defoe's classic novel to suggest the power of anti-colonial as well as colonial discourse.

Coetzee slips through the operations of various critical unfoldings of the Defoe's canonical text and sets up another text as a relatively autonomous but supplementary interlocutor, which seems to add to and substitute the original at the same time. According to David Attwell, "although it is true that his novels are nourished by their relationship with canonical Western literature, it is equally true that through his complicated postcoloniality he brings that situation to light and finds fictional forms wherein it can be objectified, named and questioned"(4-5). His works engage with a vast literary heritage and question the authority invested in precursor discourse, as well as investigate power dynamics, political oppression and ethical responsibility.

Coetzee does this by recasting both Defoe (the author) and his protagonist (Crusoe) as minor characters within a woman-centred narrative, thereby distorting and twisting the 'truths' that the reader assumes from Defoe's original. A character omitted from and silenced by Defoe's account (the female) is foregrounded in Coetzee's version through the narrator Susan, an English woman marooned for a year on the island with Cruso and Friday. The optimistic Robinson Crusoe, in *Foe*, becomes Cruso, a weak-minded mountain of insecurity who, unlike the original protagonist, lives sullenly on a desolate island with only a few tools, no gun, no Bible, no writing utensils, and no records. He labors every day to construct gigantic terraces, walled by stone, which stand empty and barren, for he has nothing to plant. In Cruso's island (as opposed to Crusoe's island), there are no providential seeds, spiritual or and natural. Such meaningless construction also symbolizes the hollowness at the core of Empire-building. Cruso as colonist manqué is not only impotent but also ludicrous.

Perhaps most significantly, Friday becomes an eccentric mute with whom the real secrets of the story exist. Further, Coetzee demystifies the racial slippage surrounding Friday. Coetzee has stated that in Robinson Crusoe, "Friday is a handsome Carib youth with near European features. In *Foe*, he is an African" (463). By transforming the light-skinned, delicately-featured Amerindian into a wooly-haired, thick-lipped, dark complexioned Negro, Coetzee makes visible the racist subtext that drives Defoe's novel, colonialism in the Caribbean, and imperialism in Africa. Reading *Foe* allegorically, then, suggests a reaction against imperialism and white supremacy. As Derek Attridge maintains, *Foe* represents

> a mode of fiction that explores the ideological basis of canonization, that draws attention to the existing canon, that thematizes the role of race, class, and gender in the process of cultural acceptance and exclusion, and that, while speaking from a marginal location, addresses the question of marginality such a mode of fiction would have to be seen as engaged in an attempt to break the silence in which so many are caught, even if it does so by literary means that have traditionally been celebrated as characterizing canonic art. (217)

While *Foe* re-writes a canonical text from marginal perspectives, it still demonstrates the power of the original to command the desire for imitation; it also exposes the silences and contradictions of the precursor text. *Foe* privileges the intersection or partial overlap between the postmodern and the postcolonial in contemporary cultures, with reference to its resistance to the monologic meta-narratives of modernism and realism (in arts), to Orientalism (in cultural anthropology), to colonialism and racism (in geopolitical history, fundamentalism and nativism) and to patriarchy (in gender relations). The novel's stylistic and ideological strategies challenge established ways of writing about race. For instance, the resolution of the plot action is an ideologically sensitive site for this challenge. It contradicts the typical ending of the colonial texts, which asserts that choice is over and that the growth of character or the capacity for defining action has ceased.

The core of Coetzee's *Foe* lies in the deconstruction of established literary styles and conventional roles assigned to blacks and women –beginning, as Silvia Nagy-Zekmi has explained in reference to feminist and postcolonial theory, "by simply subverting images of existing hierarchies (gender/class/culture/race) in a patriarchal or colonial setting"(1). *Foe* reworks Robinson Crusoe's representation of black identity in general and female identity in particular, of the values of the colonizer and those of the colonized, and of the forces of patriarchy against those who try to free themselves from it. Friday (the archetypal black man, the oppressed race) and Susan (the womenfolk) in Foe transgress social taboos, as part of Coetzee's depiction of colonized/female resistance to colonial/patriarchal power.

Although Friday seems to be an object of colonial knowledge due to his tonguelessness, he –like the black world– has his own story to tell, even if a monocultural, metropolitan discourse cannot hear it. He may seem to be an embodiment of the world of self-absorption, without self-consciousness, without the Cartesian split of self and other, without a desire; yet his silence is not an ontological state but a social condition imposed upon him by those in power. He therefore represents all human beings who have been silenced because of their race, gender and class. The apparent inaccessibility of his world to the Europeans in the story is an artist's devastating judgement of the crippling anti-humanist consequences of colonialism and racism on the self-confident white world. To Dick Penner, "Friday's muteness can be read as a symbol of the inexpressible psychic damage absorbed by blacks under racist conditions" (124). Yet his speechlessness, through negative inversion, becomes a symbol of a pre-capitalist Africa where history was transmitted and lived with full articulation, authenticity, and authority.

37

Further, Friday's muteness marks Coetzee's rejection of the canon, that is, its limited authority; this rejection takes partial shape in formal innovations and subversions of generic expectations. Throughout the novel, Friday's silence and enigmatic presence gain in power until they overwhelm the narrator at the end. Friday's detachment causes the hole in Susan's narrative, and this is the primary cause of Susan's uncertain narrative voice. In the third and final sections of the novel, Friday/the black world gains in stature as the site of a shimmering, indeterminate potency that has the power to engulf and cancel Susan's narrative and, ultimately, Coetzee's novel itself. This is an instance of the problem of closure. Friday, the radical black man, possesses the key to the ideological sensitive site of the narrative. He cannot give voice to this key, and no external discourse could adequately represent his knowledge. Coetzee does not allow Susan to assume the authority to construct the racial difference. Therefore, Susan's discourse as well as the novel's discourse, cannot appropriate the image of Africa/Africans. In frustration, Susan comments, "I do not know how these matters can be written of in a book" (*Foe* 120). Precisely, in relationship to lack of speech (Friday) and collapses of narrative voice (Susan), it is writing –specifically, writing books that challenge the literary canon– that is at stake in Foe.

Friday's own writing, that is, his marks on the slate, shows him to be the "wholly Other" (Spivak "Theory" 20); his trademark is the foot (the recontextualized foot from Robinson Crusoe and every Robinsonade). Writing is a means for him to prove that he is a human being and not an ordinary thing. For instance, Friday once installs himself at Foe's desk, assuming the position of authorship with a quill pen in hand. The embarrassed Susan intervenes and tells Foe, "he will foul your papers" (151), but Foe replies, "my papers are fouled enough, he can make them no worse" (151). This interchange upsets expectations of mastery (the white man, the white literary canon), and it has been precipitated by Friday's silent, subversive assumption of 'Western' prerogatives.

Such subversive assumptions become points of 'education' for Susan, who now believes that all races are equal: "We are all alive, we are all substantial, we are all in the same world" (152). Thus, *Foe* like much post-colonial literature rests upon one ethico-discursive principle –the right of formerly un-or misrepresented human groups to speak for and represent themselves in domains defined, politically and intellectually, as normally excluding them, usurping their signifying and representing functions, and over-riding their historical reality. The mystery surrounding Friday's silence as well as the silence surrounding Friday must be unravelled in order to allow Susan to see into the 'eyes' of the island. Friday has the ability to override both Susan's desire for authorization and Foe's ability to grant it. Friday possesses the history that Susan is unable to tell, and it will not be heard until there is a means of giving voice to Friday. This is to suggest that the world's harmony and true 'progress' will improve if there is mutual respect and cross-fertilization of ideas. Friday's voice, to wit, the black world's voice, will liberate not only himself/itself but also Susan (and, we assume, Foe the archetypal European, in other words the European world), for her story is dependent upon Friday's and the black world's meaning. Therefore, in *Foe*, the reader witnesses a gradual development towards and a concern for giving voice to the Other so long silenced in literary history. Consequently, the "subaltern has spoken, and his readings of the colonial text recover a native voice" (Spivak, "Theory" 110). In *Foe*, Coetzee uses a strategy of reading/writing that will "speak to", as distinct from "speaking for" the historically subaltern (wo)man. Although this involves an act of the imagination, it is a profoundly viable vision.

Coetzee has shifted the emphasis from the ostensibly unmediated narrative of *Robinson Crusoe* to the informing intelligence of multiple points of view. Foe wants to control the story of Susan and Friday; he is more interested in what will sell than the truth of the story. He finds the story lacking in exotic circumstances –for instance, a threat of cannibals landing on the island, as found in the original text. Susan, in her feminist temper, retorts: "What I saw, I wrote. I saw no cannibals; and if they came after nightfall and fled before the dawn, they left no footprint behind" (54). Foe, the fictional meta-author, would have preferred a replication of the story as it occurs in Defoe's text. In addition, as a racist and a misogynist, Foe wants to write the significance and meaning of Friday's (black world's) life and determine Susan's story. This is to suggest that authorship and authority are equivalent. Throughout much of the novel, however, Susan resists Foe's authority and insists on telling her own story. If stories give people their identities, and people are written by others, Susan wonders, do people really exist for themselves?

The concluding image of the novel envisions a future when people exist as full individuals and when an equal exchange will be possible among races. Susan lies face-to-face with Friday underwater, and feels "a slow stream, without breath, without interruption" (157) coming from inside him and beating against her eyelids, against the skin of her face. This is Coetzee's articulation of a strong desire for reciprocal speech from the victims of colonization, a cross-cultural dialogue. This image positively reinforces the ironic thesis developed throughout *Foe*, that African history did not begin with the continent's contact and subsequent destruction by the European colonialists. Rather than being the beginning of

African history, the colonial period signals the end of the beauty, communality and reciprocity characteristic of African culture. In the post-colonial era, it is the task of African literature to reclaim that which has been misappropriated and to reconstruct that which was been damaged, even destroyed. In fact, the tone and the narrative voice of the novel invest it with the authority to function as a counter-discourse.

Conclusion

Coetzee's *Foe* serves as a counter-text to the dominant discourse of representation in general, and to Defoe's *Robinson Crusoe* in particular. Such counter-discourse is quite justifiable because knowledge about the Other, whether seen as Oriental, as African, as Caribbean, or aboriginal, is neatly packaged and disseminated through the medium of Western literature and travelogue. Consequently, one strong reason for the emergence of postcolonial theory has been to re-think the European representations of non-Europeans and their cultures. To this end, what Coetzee –like other postcolonial African writers– has done in *Foe* is to undermine dominant notions of history by contradicting, challenging, or disrupting the prevailing discourse (Said xxiv). Yet beyond the foisted haze, the Africa that Coetzee depicts in the novel is whole, a community at peace with itself and whose pristine values are crystallized in the beauty of relationship, community and, above all, reciprocity.

Textuality should cease to be a 'battle ground' for orchestrating and illuminating the binary opposition between the colonizer and the colonized. Rather, canonical and non-canonical texts should be a means of promoting racial harmony, equality, and concord. This is in alliance with

Bhabha's opinion that textuality should have more to offer in the way of hope for the oppressed. In his words:

> Must we always polarize in order to polemicise? Are we trapped in a politics of struggle where the representation of social antagonisms and social contradictions can take no other form than a binary of theory versus politics? Can the aim of freedom or knowledge be the simple inversion of the relation of oppressor and oppressed, margin and periphery, negative image and positive image? (5)

What is needed in this millennium is the ability of disparate races and ethnic groups to come together to confront the challenges posed by globalization. Contemporary writers, scholars and critics need to articulate alternatives based on inclusivity and the full diversity of experiences. People of all ages, backgrounds and races would have a space to exercise their creativity, leadership acumen and imagination if there is an enduring racial harmony. In this way, we would be able to work collaboratively and strategically to create a world where many visions can co-exist.

Chapter Three

An African Antigone

A.Van Weyenberg

 Rejoice with us
Rejoice heartily with us
The tyrant
Who gives wicked orders
We have conquered him!
Oh yes, we have beaten him!
We have seen his back!
- Femi Osofisan, *Tegonni*

THE popularity of Antigone within Western literature, art and thought has been discussed at length, most famously by George Steiner who classifies it as "one of the most enduring and canonic acts in the history of our philosophic, literary, political consciousness" (1984 preface). At the heart of the tragedy is the conflict between Antigone, who sets out to bury her brother, and her uncle King Creon, who has issued a decree forbidding this burial.[1] Antigone's appeal largely derives from this central conflict, a conflict that appears straightforward, but on closer inspection reveals the intricate nature of the various oppositions it explores, such as that between woman and man, individual and state, private and public and the gods and mankind. Not only does this complexity make the conflict between both protagonists tragic to begin with, but it also ensures Antigone's continuing attraction as a source for philosophical and artistic inspiration.

A great number of playwrights have revisited Sophocles' original, but its contemporary popularity is particularly striking on the African stage, where Edward Kamau Brathwaite, Athol Fugard, Femi Osofisan and Sylvain Bemba have given Antigone post-colonial relevance in a variety of settings.[2] It may seem strange that African playwrights would turn to texts that represent the classical Western canon. After all, Greek tragedy originally came to colonial areas through imported, and forcefully imposed, Western educational systems, and in that sense could be seen to epitomise imperial Europe. In their seminal study on post-colonial drama, Helen Gilbert and Joanne Tompkins clarify that it is precisely this enduring legacy of colonialist education that explains the "prominent endeavour among colonised writers/artists" to "rework the European 'classics' in order to invest them with more local relevance and to divest them of their assumed authority/authenticity" (16). Still, whether or not African reworkings of Antigone should be considered counter-narratives to the Western canon is a question in need of closer investigation, and one that will be discussed later.

In this chapter we will focus on Femi Osofisan's reworking of *Antigone*, entitled *Tegonni: an African Antigone* (1994). It will first examine Osofisan's decision to draw on Antigone within the context of Nigeria. Then, it will discuss Antigone's representative value within her "new" surroundings, the (meta)theatrical aesthetics that characterise her cultural translocation and, finally, the political implications of this translocation for Antigone's status as a Western canonical figure.

The Choice of Antigone

As Kevin J. Wetmore Jr. explains in his study on African adpatations of Greek tragedy, Sophocles' *Antigone* is a play that "can be adapted into any situation in which a group is oppressed, or in which, in the aftermath of struggle, the forces of community and social order come into conflict with the forces of personal liberty" (170-171). Osofisan's *Tegonni: an African Antigone* well fits this description. It is set in Nigeria under British colonial rule, while also referring to the military dictatorships that have held Nigeria in its grip almost incessantly ever since its independence from Britain in 1960. *Tegonni* was first produced in 1994 at Emory University in Atlanta (Georgia, USA), which Osofisan was visiting during one of the most chaotic periods in Nigerian history, following the military junta's violent intervention and annulment of the presidential elections of 1993.[3] In the production notes Osofisan explains that Tegonni is intended to "look at the problem of political freedom against the background of the present turmoil in Nigeria –my country– where various military governments have continued for decades now to thwart the people's desire for democracy, happiness, and good government" (11).

The final form of the play and the idea to draw on Antigone shaped itself in Osofisan's mind when he approached Lagos airport to fly to Atlanta, driving past "burning houses, mounted placards, and screaming police and military vehicles." He writes:

> I remembered the story of the British colonisation of Nigeria and the defeat of my ancestors. And I remembered the valiant story of Antigone. The two events –one from history, the other from myth– would help me add my voice to the millions of other small voices in Africa, all shouting unheard and pleading to be set free –voices that are waiting desperately for help from friends in the free world. (10)

As this passage demonstrates, Osofisan directs Tegonni at a Western audience, but not only to appeal for their help, for he also explicitly holds Britain, France and Germany responsible for selling their conscience and supporting the military dictatorship to safeguard their economic interests (10).

Osofisan's address to the West does not mean that he absolves Nigerians themselves from responsibility for their country's crisis. At the heart of the Nigerian predicament he diagnoses a distorted consciousness that shows itself in "collective amnesia and inertia, in cowardice, and in inordinate horror of insurrection" (Revolution 15-16). It is this distorted consciousness, which is largely a distorted historical consciousness whose anaesthetic force disables change, that Osofisan sets out to heal from within. Accordingly, his theatrical practice is characterised by a critical re-evaluation of the past as a prerequisite for socio-political change in the present. Within a context of oppression, moreover, this calls for a special strategy, which Osofisan describes as "surreptitious insurrection": a way for the "dissenting artist" to "triumph through the gift of metaphor and magic, parody and parable, masking and mimicry"; a "covert and metaphoric system of manoeuvring" with which the terror of the state can be confronted and demystified (11). Performance, then, becomes such a "surreptitious" strategy by which to circumvent repression but also actively attack it.

In line with his project of re-evaluating the past to change the present, Osofisan does not set Tegonni in contemporary Nigeria but instead, turning to the root of Nigeria's predicament, situates it towards the end of the 19th century, at the height of colonial expansion. By enacting a moment of socio-political change set within this past, performance becomes a way to transform history into an active site where a renewed (historical) consciousness may start to take shape. Performance, to draw on Wendy Brown's words, thus literally "opens the stage for battling with the past over possibilities for the future" (151). Because, as Osofisan explains in a discussion of his play, *Morountodun*,

> by continuously juxtaposing scenes from myth and history; from the present and the past; and from the play's present, and the real present, ... the audience is made aware all the time of the options available, and those chosen. ... The intention is to turn the stage into a problematic space of ideological conflict, through which the audience can see itself mirrored and, possibly, energized in its struggle with history. (Theatre 9)

Another way in which Osofisan explores different ideological positions and socio-political problems is by borrowing from and challenging antecedent texts. His dramaturgy is characterised by such recourse to existing plays, both from the Western and the Nigerian theatre tradition. Thus, he engages with Samuel Beckett's *Waiting for Godot* in his *Oriki the Grasshopper* (1981), with Wole Soyinka's *The Strong Breed* in his *No More the Wasted Breed* (1982), with J. P. Clark-Bekederemo's *The Raft* in his *Another Raft* (1988), with Shakespeare's *Hamlet* in his *Wèsóò Hamlet!* (2003) and with Euripides' Trojan Women in his *Women of Owu* (2004). Osofisan gives his re-workings both local and political relevance. The first is achieved by drawing heavily on myths, rituals, songs, proverbs and parables taken from the Yoruba tradition in which he was brought up; the latter by subjecting these traditional elements to constant re-evaluation, releasing them from their possible repressive weight and granting them contemporary socio-political relevance. An example in *Tegonni* is the inclusion of the Yoruba parable of the Tiger and the Frog, teaching a moral that in the context of contemporary Nigeria acquires great political bearing: "the one who was swallowed gained a throne, while the one who usurped power fell to disgrace" (100). Tradition, then, is not treated as

47

something that is grounded outside of history or that has no political viability but, instead, as something that has a place within the (political) present; a place, however, in need of continuous reconsideration.

The Politics of Representation

The main question Sophocles poses in *Antigone* is whose claim is more "just": that of Antigone, who stays true to the laws of the gods and her private morality, or Creon, who insists on the superiority of the laws of the state and public morality instead. In a chapter on tragedy and politics, Suzanne Said explains that in 5th century B.C. Athens, such on-stage negotiation between conflicting interests and ideologies had an important didactic function, since it represented the dialectic of the political process held high in the young democracy of Athens (Boedeker and Raaflaub 282). Tragedy, then, primarily served to instruct the art of debate to audience members. In Osofisan's adaptation, written within a context of oppression that forbids such debate, the confrontation between Creon and Antigone acquires a different relevance and comes to represent the opposition between oppressor and oppressed. Within this larger field of injustice, the Sophoclean complexity of the conflict is reduced, and the ethical question of justification is rendered irrelevant. With regard to Tegonni it is therefore more constructive to think of Antigone not as the character from Sophocles' tragedy, but rather as a concept, a concept that has travelled widely through philosophy, art and literature and, while travelling, has taken on different forms, shapes and meanings.4 In Osofisan she has travelled to Africa where she becomes the representative of the struggle against oppression.

Osofisan structures his entire play along the lines of Antigone, so that the "valiant story of Antigone" (10) is transformed into that of Tegonni, princess of the imaginary Yoruba town of Oke-Osun. Creon, in turn, becomes the British colonial Governor Carter Ross, who rules the town with an iron hand. Similar to Fugard, Osofisan departs from Sophocles' ambiguous character-presentation. His Governor becomes the undisguised representative of brutal colonial oppression, a man who longs for the time when "you knew you were right, because you believed in the Cross and in the Empire" and "You hammered the Union Jack down their throats, and made them sing 'God Save the Queen'! For if you didn't do that, they would quickly resort to barbarism, to cannibalism, to living apes" (131). Sensing the dawn of a new "enfeebled" age, Osofisan's Governor obsessively clings to the historicist view that, as Dipesh Chakrabarty explains, enabled European colonialism in the first place. Since historicism "posited historical time as a measure of the cultural distance (at least in institutional development) that was assumed to exist between the West and the non-West," it was essential to the construction of colonial otherness, while it also legitimised the idea of civilisation in the colonies (Chakrabarty 7). Osofisan's Governor personifies this view and loudly proclaims that it is because people like him that civilisation acquires its destiny (131-132), though he also shamelessly states that "we're just here to give the orders, it's the niggers who do the fighting" (60).

Unlike Sophocles' Creon, who only comes to power after Antigone's brothers have died, Osofisan's Governor is actively engaged in the civil war and eagerly applies the strategy of divide-and-rule by supporting one of Tegonni's brothers with his army and treating the other as his enemy and forbidding his burial. Tegonni, like Antigone before her, disregards his decree and sets out to bury her brother's body. But the Governor represents more than brutal colonial force and also

49

refers to the military dictatorships that have held Nigeria in its grip for so many decades. Showing the ways in which the past still haunts the present, Osofisan engages with socio-political problems that are painfully familiar to his contemporary Nigerian audience, thereby calling for their active engagement. Accordingly, Tegonni is also more than the unambiguous symbol of resistance against colonial oppression, as she also becomes the agent of social and emancipatory change in a repressive traditional society.

Like Sophocles' heroine, Tegonni is presented as different, as someone who refuses to play according to the rules of the patriarchal society in which she finds herself. She is the founder of the first Guild of Women Casters and practices a trade formerly unknown and not allowed to women. Rather than propagating a return to an idealised pre-colonial past, Osofisan paints an unromantic picture of a society that not only needs to break free from colonial oppression, but also from the repressive forces of tradition. Tradition, like history, becomes something to be battled with, and Tegonni and her sisters and friends take on this battle. With regard to Osofisan's larger oeuvre, this is not surprising because, opposed to the tendency in Nigerian theatre to portray women as underdogs, almost all of Osofisan's plays portray women as agents of social reconstruction. In his view, the empowerment of women is crucial to the prospective programme of liberation and modernisation and, accordingly, many of his female characters are determined to struggle collectively to transform their society (Onwueme 25).

In Sophocles, there is no definite answer to the question whether Antigone's act of defying Creon is motivated by the desire for social change or whether it primarily stems from individual knowledge and interest. Her political reproach of Creon's "one-man rule" causing the citizens of Thebes to "lock up their tongues" would suggest the former (556). However, it is equally significant that Antigone ultimately acts alone, without the support of her fellow citizens, without the support even of her sister Ismene. Osofisan's play leaves no such ambiguity: his African Antigone, Tegonni, succeeds in unifying a group of women and her private act of defiance acquires collective relevance as it turns into a struggle for freedom from colonial oppression and for societal change.

In a way, the stark contrast between Tegonni and the Governor seems to challenge Osofisan's intention of eliciting his audience's active and critical engagement. After all, it permits an escape into the simplistic Manichean opposition of coloniser versus colonised which, in turn, reinforces rather than heals the distorted consciousness Osofisan wishes to correct. However, Osofisan moderates this opposition by including the romantic relationship between Tegonni and colonial officer Allan Jones (a relationship that is more prominent and more developed than that between Antigone and Haimon in Sophocles). Though the character Jones is set in opposition to the Governor, he does not simply embody all that is good and honourable. On the one hand, he is portrayed as sympathetic, kind-hearted and generous and, importantly, as the one who protected Tegonni when she set up her bronze casting workshop and was taken for a witch by her own people. This means that, to a great extent, Jones (the coloniser) facilitated Tegonni's (the colonised) emancipation in Oke-Osun's male-dominated society, which further complicates the opposition coloniser-colonised. But Jones is also presented as essentially powerless, too weak to stand up to the Governor, too careful to avoid confrontation and too eager to settle for compromise.

Though the love between Tegonni and Jones suggests the possibility of bridging racial, political and cultural boundaries, their marriage seems doomed from the start, and within the colonial context, their idea that it could remain outside of the political sphere seems rather naïve. The Governor, of course, does realise the marriage's political implications. His fatherly affection for Jones, echoing the relationship between Haimon and Creon in Sophocles, soon changes into a loathing for his impotence as an imperial officer: "You thought you were being a fucking hero, didn't you!" he shouts at Jones, "You'll marry a nigger woman, and show us all! Teach us a lesson perhaps about the equality of races! Rebuild the world with your penis!" (120-121). The union between coloniser and colonised and white and black symbolises a transgressive moment in history that the Governor, as the representative of Empire, is obviously not comfortable with. But neither are most people of Oke-Osun. Tegonni's sisters do wholeheartedly encourage it, but Osofisan invites his audience to contemplate for what reasons. It is interesting, after all, that the support of one of Tegonni's most committed sisters, Kunbi, seems to depend largely on the political usefulness of the marriage. She says: "Just think of what the town as a whole will gain by having a whiteman as our in-law, rather than our antagonist! We will be feared and respected by all our neighbours" (22). Through this remark Osofisan forces his audience to recognise that the opposition between oppressor and oppressed can never be neatly drawn and that resistance, no matter how committed it may be, is always to some extent informed by complicity.5

Although, as stated earlier, Osofisan reduces the complexity of Sophocles' original in making the conflict between Creon and Antigone representative of that between oppressor and oppressed, the previous analysis shows that this does not make his play simplistic. Rather, the different political context requires that different questions are posed and that complexity is to be found elsewhere. In Osofisan, this is achieved by complicating the opposition oppressor-oppressed and extending it to represent more than the binary coloniser-colonised, but also have it refer to contemporary political power structures. Additionally, rather than posing answers, Osofisan invites his audience to critically re-evaluate the past and become actively involved in changing their future.

Performing Antigone

Osofisan not only structures his entire play along the lines of Antigone, telling the story of, as the title suggest, an African Antigone, but he also metatheatrically brings Antigone on stage to interact with her African twin-sister. The word "metatheatre" encompasses all forms of theatrical self-reference, all ways in which plays call attention to their own theatricality, such as story-telling, the play-within-the-play and role-play. Gilbert and Tompkins explain that for post-colonial playwrights metatheatre holds great political potential, because it is a constructive method to engage with the politics of (self-)representation, while also offering ways to reconstruct past and present (23). Many critics analyse such metatheatrical practice in Brechtian terms, but it is important to realise that, despite Brecht's significant influence on Osofisan's dramaturgy, metatheatrical techniques are equally characteristic of indigenous African performance practices (Richards 72).

In her study on the metatheatrical device of role-play in South African theatre Haike Frank points out that the effectiveness of role-play on stage has to do with its power to confront audiences with their (different) knowledges and experiences of role-play off stage, knowledges and experiences which make them especially susceptible to recognise the performative potential of role-play to bring about change. Frank's study can be extended to any society negatively based on role definition, where groups of people are oppressed because of class, religion, sex or race, where people are forced to perform and conform to certain imposed roles. It also applies well to the Nigerian context of Osofisan. The scene from Tegonni that best illustrates this is one in which the character Antigone orders her retinue to change roles and play members of the Hausa constabulary, the army that the British raised to colonise West Africa. Experiencing that playing soldiers is "no fun at all", because all they do is carry corpses, build execution platforms, terrorise people and collect bribes, the actors soon ask Antigone for different parts, after which she promises them a scene in which they can change roles again (28-30). Antigone, then, takes on the role of theatre director and imposes roles on her attendants, roles that they do not want to perform –roles, moreover, that not only refer to the military forces in colonial times, but that will also be familiar to Nigerian viewers still experiencing military control in their daily lives. Still, this scene does more than showing the audience how different ideological positions are projected by individuals; it also presents them with the possibility of changing reality and of changing their own roles within this reality (Dunton 69-74).

Antigone's presence, then, does not remain hidden behind the mask of Tegonni, as Osofisan metatheatrically brings her on stage as a character as well. Antigone's introduction of herself is telling:

ANTIGONE: I heard you were acting my story. And I was so excited I decided to come and participate.
YEMISI: Your story! Sorry, you're mistaken. This is the story of Tegonni, our sister. Funny, the names sound almost the same, but–
ANTIGONE: Tegonni! Where's she?
YEMISI: Back in the compound there. Preparing for her wedding.

ANTIGONE: And for her death?

FADERERA: What kind of thought is that, stranger?

ANTIGONE: Antigone

YEMISI: Yes, Antigone, whatever your name is! Have you come to curse our sister?

ANTIGONE: No, oh ho. Please don't misunderstand me. I know what I'm saying. I've travelled the same route before.

(...)

ANTIGONE: Antigone belongs to several incarnations.

KUNBI: But you...you're black!

ANTIGONE: (laughs). And so? What colour is mythology?

ANTIGONE'S CREW: We're metaphors. We always come in the colour and shape of your imagination. (25-27)

This passage demonstrates that it is not Antigone the heroine from Greek tragedy who comes on stage, but Antigone the metaphor, unbound by time, place or race and willing to travel to any society in need of revolutionary change. For, as Antigone proclaims:

> Many tyrants will still arise, furious to inscribe their nightmares and their horrors on the patient face of history. But again and again, as many times as such abortions creep up, as many times will others come up who will challenge them and chase them away into oblivion. Ozymandias will rise again! But so will Antigone! Wherever the call for freedom is heard! (127-128)

Ozymandias is the name the Greeks gave to Ramses II, the Egyptian pharaoh from whom Moses and the Israelites fled during the Exodus. It is also the title of a poem on dictatorship and the fall of empires by the English romantic poet Percy Byssche Shelley (Raji 148). In the scene that follows, Antigone and Tegonni together recite this poem, while linking hands like true revolutionary twin-sisters. This image demonstrates that mythological relevance transgresses temporal and spatial barriers and emphasises that Tegonni does not exist by virtue of Antigone. In this way, the historicist view of "first in the West, and then elsewhere" is emphatically rejected (Chakrabarty 6), but does this also imply that Osofisan's engagement with Antigone should be considered as a way of writing back to the Western canon?

Beyond Antigone?

The question remains whether, in addition to an intertextual work, Osofisan's reworking of Antigone is also an example of "canonical counter-discourse", where writers develop a counter text that, by "preserve[ing] many of the identifying signifiers of the original while altering, often allegorically, its structures of power" seeks to "destabilise the power structures of the originary text rather than simply to acknowledge its influence" (Gilbert and Tompkins 16).[6] It seems strange that Gilbert and Tompkins, after first making this important distinction between works that are solely intertextual and works that are also counter-discursive, later state the following:

> Sophocles' Antigone has (…) received considerable counter-discursive attention because it disputes the state's definition of justice and champions a figure who is imprisoned for maintaining her sense of moral and legal principle. The differences between two systems of justice and the triumph of the stronger power of the weaker can easily be articulated in a colonial context. (41)

They seem to suggest, then, that articulating the power relations of Sophocles' original into a colonial context equals giving this text counter-discursive attention, whereas, according to their own definition, a counter-discursive text not only articulates, but also purposefully destabilises such power structures. Though Osofisan, like other African playwrights who draw on Antigone, reduces the ambiguity of Antigone's power structures and changes their representative value, he does not set out to counter them. And perhaps this is not so surprising, because even if we interpret Sophocles' original to stand for colonial hegemony, within this text the character Antigone, in her defiance of authority, is herself the personification of counter-hegemonic action against Creon's rule. It is precisely for this reason that Antigone has become so popular on the post-colonial stage. And it is precisely for this reason, also, that Osofisan presents Antigone as a metaphor that belongs to several incarnations, a source of inspiration for the struggle against oppression which can be conjured up "whenever the call for freedom is heard" (128). Osofisan, then, does not seem particularly interested in Antigone's cultural origin or her status as a Western canonical figure. His main concern is with her political potential in the present. It is ultimately not Antigone's foreignness but her at-homeness that is stressed.

Rather than labelling Tegonni as "counter-discursive" it seems more constructive to refer to Wetmore's "Black Dionysus" model, in which "familiarity is celebrated, but not used to erase difference" and "Greek material is seen as the original tragedians saw myth –a convenient and familiar vehicle by which one might critique society" (Dionysus 44-45). "Black Dionysus" is a

> Post-Afrocentric formulation of drama that is counter-hegemonic, self-aware, refuses to enforce dominant notions of ethnicity and culture, and uses ancient Greek material to inscribe a new discourse that empowers and critiques all cultures, even as it identifies the colonizer's power and the colonized's powerlessness. (44) 7

Still, within the context of this paper two additional remarks seem important. The first has to do with the juxtaposition of the words "power" and "powerlessness", which implies an uncomplicated binary opposition between those who do and those who do not have power, an opposition that Gayatri Spivak has demonstrated to be erroneous.8 Secondly, with regard to Wetmore's use of the term "counter-hegemonic", it is important to specify to which hegemony (or, more accurately, to which hegemonies) this term is intended to refer. After all, in the words of Osofisan, "it is nonsense to think that the hegemony in question is always the colonial/imperialist one, when the political structures of our countries are so deficient and murderous kleptocracies are in place."9

A final question remains to be answered. Because if Tegonni indeed does not exist by virtue of Antigone, how then to understand the fact that Antigone metatheatrically insists on the necessity for her story to play out exactly as it did before, for instance by hinting at Tegonni's approaching death in the first of the two passages quoted above? Though Antigone's question if Tegonni is preparing for her death does end with a question mark, it is clearly rhetorical and leaves little room to answer in the negative. And what are we to make of the fact that, as described earlier, Antigone not only comes on stage uninvited, but also takes on the role of theatre director, getting involved with the execution of Tegonni's story? A story, moreover, which in the first passage quoted above, she possessively refers to as hers: "I heard you were acting *my story*" (25, emphasis added).

In a sense, and this counts for Osofisan as well as for other playwrights who draw on Antigone within post-colonial contexts, the very emphasis on Antigone as theirs, as representing their struggle, as being relevant to their political present, inevitably embeds the dominance of Antigone's conventional representational status: as a white Western woman. In Tegonni this is illustrated by Kunbi's exclamation of surprise at seeing a black Antigone. In *The Island* by Fugard, Ntshona and Kani it is evident in the white wig on the head of the black prisoner Winston as he performs his role of Antigone. No matter how democratically available Antigone might be, her origin seems unavoidable and it is in this relation between adaptation and original that a certain inevitable ambiguity resides. By bringing Antigone on stage, Osofisan presents the illusion that Antigone is "really" there, while simultaneously stressing the distance between Sophocles' original and his African reworking. It is as if Antigone could not migrate without doubling herself. Concluding, however, it is important to emphasise that it is not Antigone's cultural and historical origin with which Osofisan is primarily concerned. It is not her past he is mainly interested in, but the political potential she has to offer for his country's future.

Contemporary Modernity

Chapter 4

Cultural Translation

K.Secovnie

Introduction

The Missing Face, like Ama Ata Aidoo's *The Dilemma of a Ghost*, addresses the topic of an African-American woman's search for her identity in Africa. In both instances, the protagonist must struggle with an African "been-to" man, educated in the United States and having returned to Africa. In each case, the man fails to adequately help the woman in her search for identity and the community itself, initially hostile to the desires of the African-American woman, comes to her aid, eventually embracing her as one of its own.

In this chapter we argue that both plays affirm the simultaneous necessity of and refusal of cultural translation. In each case, the requirement for cultural translation, which is initially unclear to the African-American women themselves, is obvious to those in West Africa, while it also becomes clear that the designated translator (the African husband/lover) has refused the mantle of translator, leaving the task to other translator figures. Specifically, the "traditional" West African mother-figures smooth the way of these African-American women into the communities they strive to inhabit. In this way, both authors redefine a Pan-Africanist agenda through a feminist emphasis on community to do the work of joining a diasporic (in this case African-American) community to

Africa. Using the theory of cultural translation described by Homi Bhabha and others, then, this essay illustrates the ways that West African dramatists have addressed the question of how to widen the frontiers of their cultures to embrace those of African-Americans and thus provide for a Pan-Africanist framework that is both realistic and effective.

Widening Frontiers?

When we speak of widening frontiers, we must acknowledge both the limits and possibilities of this paradigm. Pan-Africanism as a way to widen what it means to be African has a history that has been aptly analyzed by scholars. The problem for Pan-Africanism is the divide that often erupts between Africans and their diaspora. Here we posit that the reason for the lack of connection among groups in Africa and the diaspora is the unexamined notion that race and a common history of oppression or – in the Afrocentric scheme– a shared worldview, will automatically serve to draw disparate elements within the diaspora to "mother" Africa. This assumption of natural kinship needs to be challenged in order for true and more effective Pan-African connections to be forged and horizons widened. Frank acknowledgement of difference with the accompanying willingness to understand the view of the other and the willingness to renegotiate identity provides the framework for these burgeoning connections.

The paradigm of cultural translation provides a useful metaphor with which to examine the details of this negotiation. In his article "Translating Culture vs. Cultural Translation" Harish Trivedi describes the evolution of the phrase from its origins in linguistics: "the unit of translation was no longer a word or a sentence or a paragraph or a page or even a text, but indeed the whole language and culture in which that text was constituted" (Trivedi 3). Thus, as a metaphor, it addresses cultures as if they were different languages, in need of translation in order to be understood. Cultural translation as a construct has been taken up by some critics to theorize about the ways that postcolonial subjects find themselves, in Salman Rushdie's phrase, "translated men" (Rushdie 17). Homi Bhabha defines cultural translation as a process of imitation in which:

> the priority of the original is not reinforced but by the very fact that it can be simulated, copied, transferred, transformed, made into a simulacrum and so on: the 'original' is never finished or complete in itself. [Thus,] the 'originary' is always open to translation so that it can never be said to have a totalized prior moment of being or meaning --an essence [. . .] which makes them [cultures] decentred structures--through that displacement or liminality opens up the possibility of articulating different, even incommensurable cultural practices and priorities. (210)

We can easily see how this model relates to the former colonial subject, a subject for whom the "original" is often a nation in Europe. How, though, might the idea of cultural translation work in a situation where the original itself has been identified (in this case by the West) as a copy? This question specifically relates to the African diaspora and its efforts to form a Pan-African identity with Africa as its originary space. If we find, for instance, Black Americans looking for an originary moment in African culture, as opposed to European or American culture, how might the idea of cultural translation change? Or, when the formerly colonized look to the modernity represented by European or American culture as a type of originary model, with African-Americans as a part of that modernity, how does their identity

63

get renegotiated? In light of post-structuralism, a number of theorists have dismissed African American claims for an African-based identity, stating that identity is no longer relevant –we are all hybrids, etc. In the face of this, postcolonial theory and African American critical race theory have seemed as if they were at odds, or at best incompatible. Through the paradigm of cultural translation, however, we can see the ways in which African American identity-based theory and cultural translation and the hybridity that attends it, are not, in fact, incompatible. Indeed, the idea is explored in several pieces of West African dramatic literature which delve into how two disparate cultures (those of African Americans from the United States and those of West Africa, specifically Ghana and Nigeria) can come to understand one another and thus widen their horizons.

Ama Ata Aidoo's *The Dilemma of a Ghost* and Osonye Tess Onwueme's *The Missing Face* demonstrate the process of finding a cultural identity that does not privilege an originary moment, yet provides space for a negotiated Pan-African identity for West Africans and African Americans. Both of these plays deal with the issue of constructing a Pan-African identity through connecting African Americans with West Africans and both highlight the simultaneous necessity for and failure of cultural translation to facilitate that connection. In each play, we find a female protagonist returning to Africa only to find that the connection she initially sought was not naturally there just waiting for her. Both women (Eulalie in Dilemma and Ida Bee in Face) find the need for a cultural translation and each looks to her African "been-to" husband/lover to provide it. In each case, the expected translator fails in his duties. It is left, instead, for the West African communities themselves, led by women, to provide a translation of culture to the two African-American women that will allow them to connect with and embrace their African identity while respecting the cultures that they find in Africa (rather than the culture that they project onto Africa).

These plays, then, challenge romanticized notions of Pan-African identification through an emphasis on cultural translation and reveal the failure of the male-centered model of translation that would posit the husband as the sole translator for the wife and the "been-to" man as the sole translator for the community. Instead, a feminist agency is exerted by the West African communities in which these plays are set that undoes the western notion of translation as the domain of the male,1 and moves it into a female-led, democratic process by which the community as a whole makes decisions about how to translate itself to the diasporic culture, thus asserting a kind of indigenous African agency while privileging the role of the female within this agency. At the same time, it allows for the intervention of West African communities into shaping their own identities in new ways.

This reshaping of identity is shown in *The Dilemma of a Ghost*, the story of Eulalie, an African-American woman who has married Ato, a Ghanaian man who had been studying in the United States. The couple moves to Ghana, where Eulalie realizes that Africa is not all that she had anticipated in a homeland. Ato's family, especially his mother Esi, seem rooted in their ways and intolerant of what they see as white people's ways adopted by Eulalie and Ato in their new life in Ghana. The central conflict revolves around the family's expectation that Eulalie will become pregnant and Ato's unwillingness to entertain the idea, while he allows his wife to take the brunt of his family's criticism. When, in the end, the family, led by Esi, finds out about Ato's treachery, they take Eulalie in as their own, reprimanding Ato for his failure to uphold his values and to translate those values to Eulalie.

This embrace is not automatic, however. Eulalie initially romanticizes the idea of Africa. While still in the U.S. she and Ato have a conversation about moving to Africa where she demonstrates her lack of awareness about her soon-to-be home:

EU: I'm optimistic, Native Boy. To belong somewhere again....
Sure, this must be bliss.
ATO: Poor Sweetie Pie.
EU: But I will not be poor again, will I? I'll just be 'Sweetie Pie.'
Waw! The palm trees, the azure sea, the sun and golden beaches...
(Aidoo 244)

Although Ato initially lets her know that she has a picture out of a "tourist brochure," he also keeps her in the dark by dismissing any questions she has about his family and the new place they will be living (244). When, for instance, Eulalie expresses concern about his family's possible objection to her desire to postpone having children, Ato refuses to even entertain the idea: "Eulalie Rush and Ato Yawson shall be free to love each other, eh? This is all that you understand or should understand about Africa," he assures her (245).

While Aidoo does present Eulalie as a naïve character in some ways, she also presents a side of her that the audience would sympathize with. As Angeletta KM Gourdine points out, Eulalies "epitomizes a double consciousness: she recognizes that part of her is linked to Africa as geographical and cultural space, yet her knowledge is encoded in an Other discourse" (Gourdine, "Slavery," 33). Thus, when Eulalie first arrives in Africa, she speaks to her dead mother, saying, "Ma, I've come to the very source. I've come to Africa and I hope that where'er you are, you sort of know and approve" (Aidoo 254-255). At the same time, we are confronted with her rather ignorant views of Africa, including her idea that it is a barbaric jungle, full of drumming designed to sound the alarm for a witch hunt (255). These contrasting views show how Eulalie is identified with the discourse of the Other through her attitudes about Africa. Thus, she cannot help but cause conflict within her husband's family.

These attitudes get in the way of her forming a relationship with Ato's family in Ghana, as she does not understand their language or their customs and looks at them as rather quaint and backward. At the same time, they see her as very untraditional and cannot understand her drinking alcohol and smoking cigarettes. The central conflict, however, occurs over the issue of children, as Eulalie expected it might. Initially Eulalie wants to wait for a few years to have children and Ato agrees, but when they move to Africa she changes her mind. Ato wants to earn some money first; so he stays with the original plan. The problem comes in when Ato's entire family comes to see him to ask him if they might administer some medicines to cure Eulalie of her barrenness. Instead of telling his relatives about their decision, he chooses to say nothing, allowing his family to see Eulalie as the problem and allowing Eulalie to see his family as hostile and uncivilized.

It is at this juncture that the need for a cultural translator is fully affirmed. It seems that both cultures are at an impasse -- each unable to understand or accept the other. Ato is the obvious choice to make these different "languages" understandable, but he seems unwilling to take on the role. For instance, near the end of the play, he and Eulalie fight over his family and she insults them, calling them "bastards" and "stupid, narrow-minded savages" (Aidoo 271). Instead of explaining the reasons behind his family's behavior toward Eulalie as a good translator might, he slaps her across the face, which sends Eulalie running. When he goes to his family's compound to find her, he is forced to admit to his mother and the others that he and Eulalie were using birth control. When his mother Esi discovers this, she confronts him directly:

> Why did you not tell us that you and your wife are gods and you can create your own children when you want them? You do not even tell us about anything and we assemble our medicines together. While all the time your wife laughs at us because we do not understand such things...yes, and she laughs at us because we do not understand such things...and we are angry because we think you are both not doing what is good for yourselves...and yet who can blame her? No stranger ever breaks the law...Hmm...my son. You have not dealt with us well. And you have not dealt with your wife well in this. (Aidoo 274)

Just as Esi is reprimanding Ato, Eulalie arrives and is tenderly taken in by Esi, leaving Ato alone in the courtyard where the play ends.

Critics have variously theorized about why Ato acts the way he does in relation to Eulalie and his family. Vincent Odamtten sees Ato as representative of the "been-to" man or a sujet-en-soi who is "a paradox who, for the 'loved ones,' augurs the possibility of surmounting the restrictions and limitations of their neocolonial reality," while for those who do not receive his benefits he is a source of envy and a symbol of their oppression (31). Because Ato is a been-to, he is caught like a ghost between two worlds and his position is always tenuous. Unable to act in either direction, Ato is, in the end, paralyzed and the play ends on an unsettled note, according to Odamtten. Miriam C. Gyimah agrees with Odamtten's approach, noting that the point of depicting the masculine character of Ato as "struggling with this duality" and as "incapable of asserting a position or a reinventing of himself" is to demonstrate the "effects of colonial and masculinist exploitation" in African societies (57, 67). By contrast, Arlene A. Elder argues that "Ato's downfall is not the frequently posited, inescapable dilemma of being a 'been-to,' but that he fails to communicate the expectations of African culture to Eulalie or of African American culture to the Odumna clan. He is a faulty medium, the failed voice who should have served as intermediary between two cultures" (160). Ada Uzoamaka Azodo also affirms Ato's failure as a "culture bridge" (235).

These readings of Ato and his dilemma are important to understanding aspects of the play and also bear strongly on the idea of how to form a Pan-Africanist discourse that is sustainable and can widen the frontiers of literature and culture. Ato, as the person who knows both cultures, is responsible to serve as a kind of translator for each and yet he is continually reluctant to do so, first in America when Eulalie wants to know more about Africa and about his family, and, then with his own family when they want to know why he is not following their custom of having children after marrying. Rather than explain the ways of one to the other, he ignores the needs of Eulalie and his family and ends up alienated from both.

This situation demonstrates both the possibilities and the limits of a cultural translation between African Americans and West Africans. Aidoo recognizes both the reason for the African American longing for Africa and the lack of knowledge that they possess about the continent itself. She also feels compassion for Ato's family who, having sacrificed to support their son's American education, find him ungratefully looking down upon their traditional ways and not returning what they saw as an investment (262-3). Although the family seems unaccepting of Eulalie, it turns out that they are not, in fact, rejecting her, but are responding to the information (or lack thereof) that was given to them by Ato.

What is apparent then is that a translator is required in order for cultural contact to be possible between African Americans and Africans on the continent. Although Aidoo recognizes this need (and implicitly, its meaning for the linkages that can possibly be made between the two cultures), she is also critical of it and seeks to balance out the gendered aspects of who this translator can be (the been-to) through her affirmation of the power of the matriarch to balance the translator's possible selfish interests. In this case, it is Esi, as Lloyd Brown points out, who assists Eulalie by "recogniz[ing] Eulalie's dilemmas as a displaced black American and as a woman caught between conflicting cultural assumptions about women" (90). Esi not only recognizes her son's failure as a translator, but also fills in that gap through acknowledging the differences between her culture and Eulalie's. Thus, Esi takes her in out of compassion, as a sort of motherless child in need of help. Indeed, this is acknowledged at the end of the play when Esi states, "Yes, and I know they will tell you that before the stranger should dip his finger into the thick palm nut soup, it is a townsman must have told him to. And we must be careful with your wife. You tell us her mother is dead. If she had any tenderness, her ghost must be keeping watch over all which happen to her" (Aidoo 274). Thus, Esi affirms the role of the mother in protecting her child against the bad advice of the "townsman," in this case, her own son Ato.

Ultimately, then, Aidoo does not simply point out the failure of cultural translator in the figure of the been-to man, but also offers an alternative figure to do the work of translation--the African woman and her community. It is the "traditional" woman who sees the problem and steps in to fix the disconnection that has occurred and she holds the power to widen the frontiers of a Pan-African connection.

Like Aidoo's work, Osonye Tess Onwueme's *The Missing Face* very early on alerts the reader to the cultural conflict to come. Based on an earlier play called *Legacies*, *Face* introduces readers to Ida Bee and her son Amaechi, who have come to Africa in search of Amaechi's father Momah. Ida Bee wants her son to know his father, who stayed with her while studying in the U.S., and to embrace his African ancestry, and so they wander into the camp led by Odozi, the elder, and his wife Nebe. The first moment of misrecognition between Ida Bee and her son Amaechi and the Idu community comes when Odozi questions the strangers about who they are and where they are from. When Ida Bee is pressed for information about her lineage, she responds:

> From … from Idu…from all of Africa. We are the children of Africa…born in the new world. Africa is our land. We do not have to claim any particualar land or country because Africa was our nation…before the white man came to divide…disperse us. So why must we limit ourselves to one country…one state. No! The whole of Africa is our nationality. This is our land. We are the children of Africa. We come from here….(Onwueme 10)

After this passionate speech, Odozi responds with laughter and ridicule to the -in his view- ridiculous assertion, one which he ascribes to the "Oyibo," or white man, who "has spoilt our land" (10). He asks what he is supposed to do in the face of such a world torn apart, and Afuzue, the Town Griot, answers "continue to adjust" (11). This adage spurs the old man into thinking through the issue more deeply, recognizing the ways in which the strangers are asking him to change his own worldview: "a stranger has come to tell me that I do not know who I am. [. . .] She has come to make me Hausa, Yoruba, Bini…In my old age, I am now born again?" (11). Thus, Onwueme demonstrates how the African-Americans' quest for identity also forces the West Africans to question their own sense of self.

While Odozi is quite disturbed by this turn of events, he does not blame the strangers for their ignorance of Africa, for, as he says, "You are Oyibo. You cannot understand us" (11). Iniobong Uko notes, "Odozi is convinced that Ida Bee's inablity to comprehend these issues is because she is 'oyibo', a white person, thus signifiying that even though she is black, she is a white person, a stranger, as evident in her ignorance of African traditional values." (Uko 125) By identifying the strangers with the white man -Oyibo- he shows the distance between the two groups and identifies the lack of understanding between them and the West Africans they claim as kin (Onwueme 12).

It is clear, then, that the need for a translator -one who can understand and interpret each side to the other- is imminent. The obvious choice seems to be Momah; unfortunately, rather than serve as a link between the two groups, he is a hindrance to relations. Thus, although the cultural misunderstandings between the two groups are emphasized in the play, the real source of conflict is the failure of Momah to fulfill his role as translator. Odozi attests that this expectation was put upon his son (by leviration) early on, when the village sent him to the white man's world "so that [they could] learn his [the white man's] ways to arm and strengthen [them]selves with better knowledge" (14). While Odozi professes to the strangers that Momah has succeeded in his mission, showing himself a "true son of the soil" and, "having left behind whatever belonged to their world, that would not be good for our land", these last lines reveal an overemphasis on Momah's achievement, given that, although Momah returned many years ago from America, he is only now being initiated into manhood (14). These last lines reveal an overemphasis on Momah's acheivment, given that, although Momah returned many years ago from America, he is only now being initiated into manhood.

This becomes even more apparent later when Nebe asks the strangers to leave the shrine and they do so. Speaking to her husband, who has come to see the truth of Ida Bee's assertion, she says "Go on searching for grains of truth lost in a bag of garri! Go on! I will be the last to fold my arms when strangers come to chase my only son into the claws of the city. Momah has packed his bag ready to run back to the city. And you remember how long it took us to bring him back from the city?" (17). In these scenes, we find that the underlying problem is not so much the challenge that the strangers bring to the Idu sense of identity, but the challenge that their own son Momah brings to them. Thus, Nebe's concern that he will leave gives the lie to Odozi's earlier assertion of his son's fidelity to his clan and calls into question the sturdiness of the identity of the West African peoples themselves.

Onwueme also provides a flashback scene that reveals the Momah's true character and demonstrates his rejection of the mantle of cultural translator that his village has bestowed upon him. Instead, he has fully embraced the culture that those in the West tout as superior, while defensively asserting that Africa will one day adopt it:

> Yes, we strive to turn Africa into modern Europe. [. . .] African ways are so long and burdensome. American ways, so 'cool' and fast! A world of individualism and prosperity [. . .] We must aquire a new form of civilization. Transform the basis of our lives. Step into the 21st century walking tall. Modernize our culture. Americanize our ways. [. . .] Black-out the past. Our ancestors are nothing but archeological specimens for advanced studies on impoverished human species...Black-out the black past, backward in time and space. (29)

The above diatribe is worth quoting at length because it reveals the depths to which Momah has sunk in America. It also reveals, in a larger sense, the potential anxiety the been-to man could have about his own traditional identity in the face of an American or European modernity.

This characterization and Momah's continued unwillingness to accept Ida Bee until the very last page of the play belies Uko's characterization of Momah as "the metaphoric bridge between Idu and the New World" since, "Odozi extols him as the one whose responsibility it was to bring to Idu the benefit of the white man's world [. . .and] Momah, as the true son of the soil, fulfills these aspirations" (Uko 126). In contrast to Uko's position, we argue that, although it is true that Momah was expected to be a cultural translator, like Ato in Dilemma, he does not fulfill his role and, in fact, only makes matters worse for both his community and for Ida Bee. Clearly, there is a vacancy to be filled in the role of cultural translator, and it is Nebe who steps in to fill the gap, initiating Amaechi into the rites of manhood and, in Movement Four, performing the "Ibe ugo onu" ritual with Ida Bee, which, according to Onwueme "is an indication of love and romance from male to female, or as in this case, from any member of the family to a wife married to that family as an indication of the bond between them" (33, 36). Initiating Ida Bee into the fold, she chants, "Welcome! Welcome! Welcome Egbe! Woman...Egbe, woman-bird who does not know a land but journeys there all the same. My fellow woman...and daughter...welcome to our land..." (36). It is at this moment that Momah breaks into the scene, tells his mother to leave and proceeds to exile Ida Bee from the village into the forest of demons.

Momah's action is not without consequences, however, for Nebe later curses him, saying, "I have no son. Never had a son, nor ever will. Our son lost his manhood to woman whose breasts now swell with pride. Henceforth WOMAN shall be my song, for I can see through the eyes of woman today, the contorted brows of the land bearing the burden of tomorrow" (41). It is clear that Nebe has embraced women as the future of her land and she will not rest until she can remedy the situation with her newly-adopted daughter Ida Bee.

At this point in the play, Momah is chided by a Voice (presumably that of his ancestor, Meme) and it seems that he will finally embrace his heritage; it appears that Momah will be redeemed. Juliette Bartlett takes this view, asserting that Momah becomes more authentically African through Ida Bee's challenge to him: "She serves as a catalyst to re-acculturate with his heritage toward the end of the play when she confronts and challenges him to be more authentic" (61).

The play, then, serves as a critique of the figure of the been-to man through Ida Bee because she "serves as the reconciler between African Americans and Africans" (71). Although Ida Bee is a catalyst for change, we argue she is unable to reconcile the two groups, since she is implicated in the conflict and, by the end of the story, is not even in her right mind, having been cast into the evil forest by Momah. This is further confirmed as Momah's lecture to his son Amaechi is interrupted by the appearance of the two women. Nebe, who "emerges rather frantically" from the forest with her face showing that "she has been searching for too long" and Ida Bee, seemingly out of her mind from her time in the forest, disrupt the narrative of redemption that might have been offered to Momah (Onwueme 55).

While Nebe desperately tries to bring Ida Bee back from the brink, she also condemns her son openly, saying, "See the destructive handiwork of man! How I wish I knew it would come to this. MOMAH! Oh! It's MOMAH's doing" (56). She then turns her attention to understanding and interpreting Ida Bee's strange actions, eventually realizing that the Ikenga that Ida Bee carries was given to her by her father, having been passed down by their mutual ancestor Meme. The dramatic final scene results in the matching of the two halves of the missing face, one held by Momah, which was apparently left upon the footpath while their great grandfather Meme was being taken captive, and the other provided by Ida Bee. Nebe plays a key role in restoring order after the village recognizes the kinship of these two "strangers" with the community itself and, as Onwueme writes, "Nebe recovers and walks over to the loom. She sits down and begins to weave. Ida Bee slowly disengages herself from Momah. She walks over to join Nebe at the loom. The two women begin weaving together" (59). The scene ends with Amaechi and Momah once again lifting the two pieces of the Ikenga together in the air, symbolizing the joining of the two communities.

The fact that Nebe and Ida Bee end the play weaving together is significant to our thesis which sees Nebe as the lead cultural translator in the drama. It is, once again, she who takes the role in solving the mystery of Ida Bee's identity. She also embraces Ida Bee even before she realizes their literal kinship, on the basis of her own realization of the unity of the two women despite the differences in place and time that had separated them. She realizes that the true separating factor is not so much culture as her own son, whom she rejects when she realizes his complicity in destroying the Idu world. Instead of simply falling victim to this fate, however, she steps up and takes the initiative to draw the strangers into the fold of the community, and thus provides an example for her son and others to follow.

Nebe is described in the cast of characters section as "(56 years old): Mother to MOMAH and wife to ODOZI. 'Nebe' --

'We Watch the World' (Onwueme 1). She sees the world, which could be taken to mean the world both within Idu and beyond. This ability to see beyond what others see gives her a leading role as a translator figure for the play, though she also shares it with the community at large.

Of Nebe, whose name in the earlier version of *The Missing Face*, is Anene, Mabel Eveirthom writes:

> Elozie's [Momah's] mother is a character who stands for the maintenance of tradition, and this trait makes her stand out in the text. [. . .] Anene's character complements that of her blacksmith husband (by leviration) Baadi [Odozi], who fully accepts the returnees as children of Idu, while she advocates for their expulsion at the initial part of the play. [. . .] One could wager that Anene voices the writer's ideological stand, although one wonders why this role is not adequately developed in the play, and why Anene should be the character for such a purpose. (202)

Anene's characterization remains much the same in the later play and looking at Nebe as a cultural translator helps to answer Eveirthom's query: Nebe not only voices Onwueme's ideological stance, but she enacts it, which reveals her purpose in the play -to bring the two cultures together.

Thus, like the figure of Esi in *Dilemma*, Nebe, the "watcher of the world" is the person who fulfills the role not taken up by the heir-apparent to the mantle of cultural translator. Through her embrace of the role, she is able to reconcile the two cultures, integrating the African Americans into her own Idu culture through her leadership in the community. Because she is one of the larger African 'traditional' community, and not the worldly been-to that her son is, she is able to access a translation of one culture to another and, through her compassion, rescues the African American woman from the harm her former lover wishes on her.

77

Although his focus is Legacies, Chris Dunton expresses some doubt about what happens after the reconciliation, writing, "there is a failure to establish with any conviction the structure of a society that will maintain its traditions and yet reabsorb the travellers from the West" (106). This concern could also arise in *The Dilemma of a Ghost*, where the play ends without a glimpse of everyday life after the crisis. This essay argues that this concern, however, is one that would ultimately be mitigated with the ascension of the mother as translator figure. Presumably, relations cannot and will not be the same with the taking on of the translator role by the mother figure, rather than the figure of the been-to son, the one who, as Ida Bee puts it earlier in the play is "so undefined" (Onwueme 28). One imagines that the chastised figures of Ato and Momah will continue to struggle with their identities, but that the Esi and Nebe may be better equipped to handle their own struggles, and thus, with understanding, patience, and compassion will continue to serve in their role as cultural translators, easing the otherwise fraught transition of the African American characters into their adopted communities.

These two plays, then, show the way that cultural translation is both a necessity and a danger to Pan-Africanist relationship. In both instances, it is at once required, rejected by what would seem to be the obvious choice (the been-to husband or lover), and taken on by a member of the "traditional" West African community. The fact that in both cases, the mother of the errant son is the leader in taking on this mantle suggests a radical altering in the way that identity is posited in these plays and leaves space for a more feminist community-based identity to flourish. But, one might ask why this particular metaphor might be important to use in describing these relations? Why not some of the other metaphors used to describe this formation of community?

In *The Difference Place Makes*, for instance, Angeletta Gourdine argues:

> Understanding 'the difference place makes' made a bridge the only logical chronotype for the analyses I undertake, [. . .] Functionally, the writers and their writing bridge the Middle Passage. (103-104)

Gourdine's attention to the metaphors used to describe the relationship is vital, but caution should be used in foregrounding "place" in terms of a physical geography, since it assumes a possible melding with the idea of nation that can be difficult to disengage from. In the work of Aidoo and Onwueme, for instance, the insistence is less on a particular place than on the situation of time and its relation to the present. Thus, in both plays we see inquiries into the ancestors of the African American visitors, neither of whom, because of the distance that time has created, can adequately answer the questions. This provides the central conflict around which a redefinition of diasporic identity comes into play, pulling into the equation the need for a cultural translation, and initiating what will be the central motif of each play, which is the radical shift of the figure of translator to that of the "traditional" African woman, who can connect one cultural "language" to another and smooth the way for an integration of the diasporic and the "originary" self.

Gourdine is not the only one to use the metaphor of the bridge, however. As noted earlier, some critics have seen Ato's role in *Dilemma* as being like a bridge. While he could be thought of in terms of a cultural bridge between the two groups, albeit a faulty one, this metaphor lacks applicability in a situation wherein the two cultures are not, in fact, land masses which are static and unmoving, but people who, through time, interaction (both with colonial powers and with one another) have ever-shifting allegiences, situations, and needs. Thus, the bridge metaphor is itself shaky and may be part of the problem with presenting the 'been-to' man in such a manner. Lakoff and Johnson, in *Metaphors We Live By*, suggest that the conceptual metaphors that undelie the way we speak about abstract concepts such as culture help to determine the very way we think about those concepts, since, "much of cultural change arises from the introduction of new metaphorical concepts and the loss of old ones" (145). Our proposition of the metaphor of Esi and Nebe as cultural translators, then, seems to better suit the positions of each side, since it allows each to find in the other a type of moveable source and, in doing so, helps to renegotiate identity to improve the lot of both parties. The fact that both women's sons fail as translators suggest that the role needs to be taken on by characters who are more flexible, more able to "continue to adjust". What this metaphor offers, then, is an open-ended solution to the problem stated at the start of this essay --how does an "Other" look to another "Other" for self-definition? In each case, the two cultures are disparate and yet understandable to one another -but only with the aid of a cultural translator. Aidoo and Onwueme make a radical move in insisting that a new metaphor requires new actors to widen the identity horizons of Africans both in the diaspora and in the Continent.

Chapter Four

Poetics of Diaspora

J.Westmoreland

"La ca't de séjou', plus fort que la minute de silence dont on fit une symphonie, que l'Empire State Building filmé en continu pendant huit heures, que le pot doré de Beaubourg, et que les frigidaires superposés." (Bessora 29)

A NEW poetic and literary trend among Francophone African diasporic authors, specifically those writing from Paris, is the use of surrealist techniques in a "postcolonial" context. This practice dates back to Negritude's affiliations with such European surrealist writers as André Breton. Whereas traditionally in African diasporic context, Surrealism has been used to articulate a sense of solidarity or belonging (as in the formation of the Negritude and Black Power movements), Bessora employs surrealist imagery in the immigrant context to articulate a sense of unbelonging or anxiety-filled, hybrid state of the female immigrant in Paris.

In her semi-autobiographical novel *53cm*, the Swiss-Gabonese writer, Bessora, satirizes the exaggerated significance of the various "cartes" that will permit her protagonist, Zara, to become part of the French Nation through the acquisition of citizenship. In ironic tones, she fetishizes these seemingly unattainable objects, thus underscoring the absurdity of the immigrant situation as created by the French government. The contradictions inherent in the immigrant position are clearly manifest in the continual adherence to a false hope: becoming a French citizen despite the impossibility of attaining the requisite "cartes." By fetishizing the cartes, Bessora inflates their importance to the point at which they become absurd. In the case of Zara, it is not necessarily the carte itself that is ridiculous but the legal processes and rigorous physical rituals one must undergo in order to obtain the desired status of citizen.

In this quest, Zara is forced to negotiate not only complex bureaucratic obstacles, but also physical ones as she forms her body into the "condition" required by the nation. As Zara explains it, acceptance into the French nation is highly conditional, based on the correct "condition" of not only the body but of one's identity itself. Therefore, to become "French" not only the normalization of the body is required, but the normalization of one's identity as well. In this case, the hybrid or impure identity of the immigrant (the ultimate sign of alterity) must be transformed in order to gain access to the nation. According to Zara, the two cartes one must obtain in order to acquire the carte d'identité (the signifier of French citizenship) are the carte de séjour (resident visa) and the carte de gym (gym membership):

> J'ai conlcu un contrat avec le diable, grimé en troglodyte souriant à peau de girafe. Je tressaille. Mais…je dois continuer sur la voie de la cartographie. J'ai la ca't du Gymnasium; Il me faut subtiliser une ca't de séjou', et additionner ces deux ca't pour obtenir une ca't d'identité vichyste. (53)

Throughout the narrative, Bessora refers to these cartes in what surrealist thinkers would describe as a convulsive manner, constantly repeating and mutating their titles until the objects themselves are stripped of all rational qualities or "official" status. In doing so, she critiques the impossibility of fulfilling the expectation of the French nation. Framing her work in a surrealist understanding of the fetish and convulsive repetition, one can trace the representation of these cartes throughout the novel and examine their significance (or lack thereof) in terms of citizenship, belonging, and normalization of both body and identity. Bessora uses these surrealist techniques not only to counter the official French discourse and deflate the importance of the "carte," but also to open up the possibility of new narratives and associations coming out of the immigrant experience.

Before beginning an analysis of Bessora's discussion of the cartes in *53cm*, let us situate her corpus within a larger surrealist context. Certain texts, namely her short story "The Milka Cow," have been described as "fantastic." In the introduction to an anthology of short Francophone stories entitled From Africa, Adele King describes "The Milka Cow" as "(leaving) politics aside for a fantasy voyage." (King 16). The fantasy world she creates in this short text is accomplished using a surrealist mode, juxtaposing two systems of representation until they meld into one illogical, "hybrid" field of signifiers.[1] Though not all fantasy can be categorized as surrealist, the techniques used in this text to generate Bessora's fantastic setting in "The Milka Cow" are highly influenced by surrealist thought. However, it is important to note that Bessora does not outwardly claim to be part of a particular nouveau-surrealist movement. For this reason, we would not classify her texts as surrealist, rather as being informed by surrealist modes of expression. A reading of *53cm* through a surrealist lens reveals certain nuances of the "cartes" or "ca't" that would not necessarily be exposed in another interpretation (be it realist or Other). In the context of

53cm, Bessora's use of Surrealism is a mode of resistance against hegemonic culture or dominant modes of representation. Her work falls under the category of counter discourse defined here by Françoise Lionnet:

> Dominant systems are more likely to absorb and make like themselves numerically or culturally "weaker" elements. But even the "inferior" or subaltern elements contribute to the evolution and transformation of the hegemonic system by producing resistances and counter discourses. (9)

Zara resists absorption into the dominant culture by emphasizing and maintaining her hybrid position (and thus her alterity) throughout the novel. Her surrealist counter discourse proposed in 53cm serves to expand the reader's understanding of the immigrant position regarding French citizenship. Different from Bessora's use of surrealist modes in "The Milka Cow," *53cm* does engage with overtly political themes. Bessora is not alone in her practice of using Surrealism to elucidate certain socio-political paradoxes. Since the Césaires and the *Tropiques* journal,[2] Surrealism has been used to subvert dominant paradigms in the postcolonial francophone setting. As T. Denean Sharpley-Whiting notes:

> On an artistic level, Surrealism rejected aesthetics, moral concerns, and literary and artistic values as elitist, repressive, and requiring conformity. Such values and ideas clashed with the Surrealist credo of calling into question "reality"--which was seen as essentially rooted in exploitation and inequality-- with the hope of creating a "superior reality," a sur-réalité...The mind was to be freed of rationalism, logic, reason, and Cartesian philosophy, the supposed cornerstones of Western bourgeois culture and ideology, which occasioned auto censorship and repression of basic drives. (84)

In the case of Bessora, this use of Surrealism is contrasted with the exclusive and limiting role of the French State, a system that seeks to impose a homogenized identity. Whereas the State accepts only one sort of "pure" identity, Surrealism relies on the merging of systems and hybrid constructions to achieve a "sur-réalité," or alternative understanding of the situations at hand. The purity desired by the French nation is made clear at the beginning of the *53cm* at the moment Zara finds herself in "le règne gymnasial." She observes a young Arab man on a treadmill in the process of purchasing a purebred feline: " –Merde... j'ai brûlé que 42 calories. Quoi? Mais non ma chérie! Le singapora est une race félinidée découverte par les Américains dans les égouts de Singapour; un pur-sang de race hyperpure, oui." (Besora 11). Here, the feline is only accorded value after it is "discovered" by the Americans (another colonizing power) in the sewers of Singapore. The "pure" creature is rescued and brought to civilization through an act of economic interest. Her value is analogous to that of the "pure" African female (not one of mixed origin like Zara). The "real" African symbolizes (or at least did at one time) cultural capital and exotic value in the Parisian center. Like the African woman (rescued by the French from the depths of Africa), the Singapora is desired not only because she is exotic, but also because she is pure. This passage underscores the impossibility of entering into the Nation if one is métisse. Purity is clearly associated with bodily perfection in the context of the "gym," thus emphasizing the stringent requirements for citizenship.

Bessora's choice to counter the notion of purity using surrealist techniques is quite logical if one examines the basic tenants of surrealist thought. Michael Richardson emphasizes not only the hybrid nature, but also the cosmopolitan qualities of Surrealism:

In Surrealism, the universal is conceived in a multiplicity of forms. Within this relation, specific cultural identities are constantly being formed as part of a complex mosaic that makes up any human being. For it should go without saying that all cultural traditions are hybrid, bringing together disparate elements to form an unstable whole, one that necessarily disintegrates under close analysis. (Richardson 83)

French citizenship is a very exclusive category that demands purity from its members, even if this purity is falsely constructed out of a fictionalized French history.[3] It is a society based on reason and logic, one that is based on the concept of a monolithic universal identity, whereas Surrealism permits the universal to be constructed in a multiplicity of forms. In her article on [53cm], Patricia-Pia Célérier uses a quote from Voltaire's *Candide* to emphasize the importance of Cartesian thought for the French and the ways in which Zara (as a hybrid identity) could never fit into the paradigmatic requirements of French citizenship.

Le racisme est rationnel et cartésien, la Raison et la race dirigent le monde; ils sont le moteur de l'histoire universelle." (Candide). Les choses fonctionnent comme ci les réalités postcoloniales (immigration, économie globale, métissage, etc.) entraînaient une reconception de la notion de "race" et de ses applications, mais en fait les bases épistémologiques qui informent la conduite des affaires nationales sont restées similaires. En quête de carte de séjour, Zara représente cet écart. (Célérier 75)

The use of the term "quête" (not only by Célérier, but also by Bessora herself) when discussing Zara's relationship to the carte de séjour is indicative of surrealist practice. At various points throughout the text, Zara refers to herself as an "ethnologue." To support this claim, the very structure of the novel reads like an ethnographic document.[4] This stylistic mode is significant in that it subverts the European ethnographic gaze (on the Other), thereby making "official" French culture the object of analysis or exoticization. As Célérier indicates:

> Pourtant, chevillés sur une lecture critique de l'anthropologie, les romans de Bessora ont un aspect plus subversif car ils rendent exotiques les Français "de souche" et ainsi, éclairent et repoussent plus efficacement les processus "d'exotisation" des "gens de couleur." (Célérier 75)

This practice of reverse exoticism is significant in the surrealist context. The surrealists critiqued exoticism (primarily in the colonial context)[5] as a practice that assumed and emphasized the inferiority of the colonies. However, the surrealists did fetishize certain "primitive" objects in their writing and artistic interpretations. This practice could be read either as a contradiction or as a distinguishing between exoticism and the practice of fetishization.

The fetish is, by definition, an element imbued with a certain level of importance (often spiritual in nature). It is usually foreign, meaning that in an ethnographic mode a culture's fetish is usually identified by an outsider looking in.6 In Surrealism, the fetish typically appears in the context of the journey (often psychic or imaginary). One of the most recognized surrealist fetishes is the female body, made famous by the photographs of Man Ray. In *53cm* the "pure" or perfect female body is fetishized not because it holds some sort of final value, but because it leads to the acquisition of French citizenship. Lionnet comments on the importance of purity in the following passage: "Difference then becomes —on both sides of this binary system– the reason for exoticizing, 'Othering,' groups that do not share in this mythic cultural purity" (14). Zara is regarded as Other in the eyes of the French because she lacks purity of both body and identity. Adopting an ethnographic analytical position, she reverses the traditional gaze (center toward the periphery) by fetishizing elements of the dominant system (the cartes). As these excerpts exemplify, this ethnographic approach serves to further objectify this relationship between the carte and identity:

> L'accès à la Gaule, vous le savez, exige un long et pénible détour: l'escalade du mont préfectoral. Un temple de dresse sur son sommet, centre des étudiants étrangers. Mon premier dessein sera d'y pénétrer pour dérober un talisman appelé ca't de séjou'. (Bessora 29)

> En échange du papier, l'officiante donne le talisman, ca't de séjou'. Il protège de mille oiseaux volants, charters, qui boutent les explorateurs hors de la tribu, dans le plus grand secret. Cat' de séjou' protége aussi d'esprits vengeurs et innombrables, nommés Police, comme l'Eunuque aux cheveux longs. (33)

In both passages, the italicized carte is exoticized through lexical gestures to the foreign element. It is imbued with a sort of spiritual significance through references to the temple, the pilgrimage, and the talisman. In this case, Zara's fetishization of the cartes can be read through a satirical lens. She does not fetishize them to exemplify their importance. Rather, by employing this exaggerated discourse, she is satirizing their importance to the French nation. Not only is the carte "fetishized" by Zara, but in another obvious clin d'oeil to Surrealism, it is displayed as a found object art piece in the style of Marcel Duchamp.

Avec la cat' de séjou' j'entends révolutionner l'art contemporain, inventer mon genre à moi, toute seule. Chère cat' de séjou, ton compte est bon: je saurai faire de toi une oeuvre d'art, car la valeur de l'art, c'est le dollar. L'expédition terminée, je tirerai un bon prix de ta vente à un musée d'art modèrne. À moi Beaubourg, le Guggenheim, le MOMA de New York et le MIKO de Kyoto; si l'art ne veut de moi, un musée- cimitière te conservera, toi l'objet mort, tel un vieil appendice dans un bocal plein de formol. Ou alors, le Muséum d'histoire naturelle t'empaillera. Tu seras très bien, entre les restes d'une girafe et le cadavre sans sépulture d'une vénus hottentote. (Bessora 29-30)

The placement of the carte in a museum as a found object further strips it of its official significance (as recognized by the French government). For the Surrealists, the importance of the found object was not the object itself, but the conceptual dialogue that surrounded it. In the same way, Bessora devalues the actual carte in favor of the various social issues it allows one to address. By aligning the carte with the surrealist notion of found object, she is opening up the possibility for counter discourses, led by immigrant voices themselves, that challenge dominant notions associated with the carte, specifically the rhetoric of purity, full assimilation, and the impossibility of hybrid identities that has historically been imposed by the French government. In the second half of the passage, the carte is not placed in a space where it could even be accorded the status of "art". It is a forgotten relic in a museum of history. More importantly, it is misclassified, thrown next to another forgotten history, that of the Venus Hottentot. In addition to this excerpt, Bessora problematizes the practice of categorization throughout her discussion of the cartes. One of the most basic tools of classification is the label, or the Saussurian signifier. In the case of the cartes, Bessora changes the signifier all together (from "carte" to "ca't"), thus allowing for a completely different set of signifieds or associations.

Throughout the novel, Zara plays with the official language associated with the "carte," referring to it as "ca't". She repeats this term frequently throughout the text and constantly refers back to the carte to demarcate the passage of time. Whether Bessora is consciously referencing (or employing) the surrealist practice of convulsive repetition is not clear. However, reading these passages from this perspective further reinforces the complexity of her relationship to the cartes and what they represent to the hybrid or "impure" identity. The surrealists used the term convulsive when referring to aesthetics, often associated with the term beauty. This concept appears in writing for the first time in Breton's *L'amour fou*:

> Le mot "convulsive", que j'ai employé pour qualifier la beauté qui seule, selon moi, doive être servie, perdrait à mes yeux tout sens s'il était conçu dans le mouvement et non à l'expiration exacte de ce mouvement même. Il ne peut, selon moi, y avoir beauté- beauté convulsive- qu'au prix de l'affirmation du rapport réciproque qui lie l'objet considéré dans son mouvement et dans son repos. (32)

This particular passage applies well to the immigrant situation. Here, the "objet" could be read as the carte or as the immigrant herself. In the context of the immigrant, "mouvement" and "repos" could be read in terms of advancement. In order to advance, the immigrant must acquire the appropriate cartes. However, to eventually arrive at a place of "repos" (having finally acquired the carte d'identité), Zara must continually move[7] to form herself into the identity accepted by the nation, even if the impossibility of ever reaching at this resting point is evident. Ironically, the absence of the cartes needed for this transformation (here, one may think specifically of the carte de gym) forces her into a state of stagnation (a forced "repos") at various points throughout the novel.

As if attempting to combat this stagnation, Zara repeats certain terms and themes. This constant activity (or psychological movement) could be examined under the rubric of convulsive beauty. The Surrealists, namely Breton and Aragon, used a strategy of convulsive beauty to "hystericize" aesthetic, social, and ideological norms by calling all such assumptions into question. According to their definition, hysteria is precisely that which escapes definition. For the surrealists, hysteria was not uniquely a pathological phenomenon. Rather, it was in every respect a supreme means of expression. Zara's hysteric repetition of the word "ca't" and the (convulsive) frequency at which she mentions the term call into question the "normalcy" of not only the carte, but the systems though which one must pass to obtain it. The concept of convulsive repetition also applies to Bessora's recurrent obsession with the body (and normalization of it) throughout the novel. Though she refuses to conform to the bodily ideal, either of "Frenchness" or of the "Other" (the stéatopyge), she constantly makes references to her own body to the point of obsession ["Mes fesses ne poussent pas."] (Bessora 60).

The repetition of the word "carte" and the various word associations to follow ("ca't," etc.)8 call into question the rational significance of the carte. Adding yet another layer, Bessora creates a new terminology for the cartes that "creolizes" the official titles. The use of Créole is significant for two reasons. Though Zara is of Swiss-Gabonese origin, it is assumed twice in the novel that she is from the Antilles. The underlying notion here is that all immigrants are the same (that is to say, impure) until their identity is normalized by the state. It also calls into question dominant assumptions about race, skin color, and origin. By creolizing these titles, Zara not only satirizes the official status of the carte, but illustrates how the "official" carte is paradoxically slippery, elastic, and hybrid, lending itself to multiple readings and meanings depending on the context and the reader.

In the following passage, Zara references the "ca't de c'éolité", a fictional construct: "Tu parles français, mais l'interprète du tribunal traduit quand même: tu as oublié de fournir ta fausse ca't de c'éolité 'moi y en a pa'lé beaucoup bon f'ançais mon commandant'" (Bessora 68). According to the State, no foreigner could have sufficient mastery of the French language, thus a translator must be present. Again, Créole is chosen as the default immigrant tongue since, with its multiple influences, it is antithesis of a "pure" language.

Zara's status as "étudiante" and "mère" serves to further negate her purity in the eyes of the Nation. When she visits the immigration office to attempt to acquire papers for her daughter, she is systematically denied. The reason for this is not that her daughter is unfit to enter the Nation, but that workers find it unfathomable that Zara could be both a student and a mother:

> L'OMI n'a rien demandé à votre enfant, parce que les étudiants étrangers n'ont pas d'enfants. Ils viennent en France pour faire des études et rentrer chez eux, pas pour faire des enfants et rester en France. Nous n'avons donc plus besoin du certificat OMI: vous êtes étudiante étrangère, célibataire et sans enfants. (68)

Thus, Zara is ultimately hybrid (in race, role, and identity). Her race is mixed (Swiss and Gabonese), and she occupies a specific hybrid social position for which the French have no "carte" (that of "étudiante-mère"). In her refusal to deny her hybridity not just culturally (suisse-gabonaise), but socially (étudiante-mère) she reveals the impossibility of both obtaining the carte and retaining one's own identity. Her particular identity is based on an image of transplantation rather than rootedness, as is discussed at her first visit to the OMI: "Vous vous nommez Zara S...Sem...Andock; vous êtes née le 25 décembre 1968 à Bruxelles, d'une mère Suisse nomade et d'un père fang gabonais? Mais qu'est-ce que vous faites en France?" (28). This last line underscores the impossibility of retaining such an identity if one wishes to become part of the Nation.

The carte d'identité imposes a pure, French identity and forces one into a state of fixedness. In the eyes of the State, you are French or you are nothing. The possibility of a hyphenated identity does not exist. This stasis implies control over one's identity, both physical and psychic. Each citizen of France (naturalized or "français de souche") must carry the carte on his or her person at all times. "Le contrôle" is the official term for the act of being stopped by government officials to verify possession of the carte. Thus, to a certain extent the French State is continually perceived as watching the activities of its inhabitants. This "contrôle" is one of the greatest sources of anxiety for the illegal immigrant, who does not possess the proper "identité." In this way, the "contrôle" serves as a Foucaultian panopticon.[9] Even if it never actually happens, the threat of the "contrôle" is always present.

Although Bessora uses surrealist modes to satirize the "ca't," her protagonist remains in a bind. The carte is still important to Zara not only for her own survival (or success), but also for that of the person who complicates her identity most profoundly, her daughter. Though she is able, through her surrealist interventions, to distance herself psychologically from the importance given to the carte (by the Nation), she is unable to escape her eventual dependence on it. For very real and tangible reasons, the carte d'identité is necessary in order to access the means to live (or thrive) in the Metropole.

Bessora's text is not the first to deal overtly with the issues of bureaucracy and the carte d'identité in the postcolonial context. Rather, it is a part of an extended thematic trend. Here, one is primarily referring to texts such as Ousmane Sembene's Le Mandat and Jean-Michel Adiaffi's La carte d'identité, both of which take place in Africa and feature African male protagonists who experience many of the same frustrations, injustices, and problematic dependence on official governmental documents as Bessora's Zara.[10] By resituating the dialogue surrounding the carte in a feminine narrative, Bessora engages with the power struggles and feelings of physical or cultural inadequacies from the perspective of the diasporic woman. Relying on humour, satire, and discussions of naming, Sembene and Adiaffi's novels ask the reader to consider what identity is for the postcolonial African. While each of these elements are found in 53cm, Bessora shifts the discussion to a new geographical and gendered space, preparing a complex web of power dynamics and bureaucratic tensions that are never fully resolved. Reading Bessora's *53cm* in concert with such realist representations of the carte situates this text in a geneology of postcolonial narratives that underscore the anxieties surrounding the acquisition of French identity and acceptance signified by the "cartes" whether real, imagined, or ideological.

Chapter Five

The Rhetoric of Despair

O.Okuyade

Do you wonder why the Lord of the Rock
still possesses millions of worshippers
despite the bloodstained soil on which they kneel?
The Lord has hired a crop of fortune-tellers,
the gifted children of his victims, to counsel
that more human offerings need to be made
to ensure that he lives and rules forever.
If you accuse the Chieftain of being an evil idol,
don't spare his tribe of willing worshippers;
they share the same monstrous faith.
(Tanure Ojaide: *Delta Blues & Home Songs*)

Introduction

OUR discourse is centred against the background of public attitudes and orientation towards military or democratic governance in Africa. It evinces the relationship between political and legal sovereignty in Chin Ce's *Children of Koloko*, a book that artistically anatomizes the Nigerian society in its grossest sense in order to give the reader a proper understanding of that society. African literature is hardly discussed outside contemporary history from where it derives its pre-occupation. From the late 1970s till date, African literature continues to be inward looking, x-raying the entire

95

continent with the people trapped in serious socio-economic crisis. According to Chidi Amuta:

> it is indisputable that national history and national social experience furnish a thematic quarry and an ideology imperative in the context of which African writers have been working, especially in the post-colonial period. Individual African writers have consistently testified to this fact in both their polemical utterances and literary creativity. (62 63)

To assess African literature more effectively, critics must take into cognizance that this artistic vocation is a recreation of social realities and a critique of the African condition. African writers are alert and alive to their responsibility not only as teachers but, as Oyeniyi Okunoye puts it, "critics and chroniclers of shared experiences" (19). They continue to appraise the ruling class thereby signposting the failures of post-colonial nation states.

The post colonial African terrain has been a turbulent geography since the 1960s when independence began to sweep through the continent. As the ruled continue to falter even within the marginal space where they are being held supine, so do their rulers progressively plunge them into poverty with the apparatus of power permanently confiscated for public subjugation. The disenchantment with Africa's independences has made most African writers identify with the people's efforts to resist the rulers. In Josaphat Kubayada's words:

> Postcolonial dictatorship in Africa concerns itself with repression, which in effect means the arrest, exile, execution, or consistent harassment of dissident voices. The general result of dictatorship is an atmosphere of fear, hate and humiliation. (5)

At present the nation-state in Africa continues to wobble in crisis of varied dimensions. Political misrule and corruption become the major indices by which African rulers are identified. This has provoked widespread skepticism about the function and relevance of government, which in turn has led to public resignation in the belief of the dream of a better tomorrow. The sense of despair it evokes prompts African writers to allegorize this big burden of Africa. Patrick McGee contends that this allegory "arises from a culture in which the real world has become meaningless, devoid of intrinsic value, fragmented yet mysterious" (241). The African writer seems frustrated as (s)he watches the rulers toy with the collective aspirations of the people. Disillusioned by the wave of dictatorships that have obstructed any form of development on the continent or contributed to the gradual disintegration of their nations, the continent becomes a necropolis in which, according to Jean Franco, "[individual] and collective identity, social and family life [are] like shells from which life [has] disappeared" (205).

The novel is the most popular of the three genres in Africa, primarily because of its essential feature which concedes an elaborate plot with which to capture the aspirations and fears of the people. However, the African writer does more than story telling. Helen Chukwuma argues that the novelist "arouses in the reader a true sense of himself, evoking his past and linking it to the present" (vi). For the African writer, the challenges of approximating and representing the socio-political events in the society in his/her imaginative craft go beyond mere story telling. It has to do with his ability to transform the social statistics in order to harmonize the problems of society and the writer's commitment to his/her artistic vision.

Rhetoric and Narrative in Children of Koloko

Chin Ce's biggest asset in *Children of Koloko* is his ability to describe characters and scenes so vividly, and, by these descriptions, appeal greatly to readers' senses thereby creating a sense of presence and immediacy in the story. This outstanding element of style comes across in the lucid flow of language and the linearity of his plot narrative. Though the stories are told from the first person narrative perspective, the novelist is able to enter imaginatively into the emotional streams of other characters and, by the use of simple evocative words, record his observations with poetic lyricism and dramatic immediacy.

The narrative of *Children of Koloko* covers almost every aspect of life and governance, but the leadership factor underlies the literary substance of the novel. The problem of leadership hovers over everything in the narrative and hence becomes the source of societal tragedy. Among the people of Koloko we encounter an experience: an experience of a living world that is slowly dying. Ce lucidly cartographs the familiar anguish that surrounds the exclusion of African masses from the common wealth –the prodigal desire of their daily lives. The book becomes a parable on the Nigerian situation where power is consolidated in a few hands and they run away with politics which is achieved by demagoguery and deceit. Said Khamis sees this as "characteristic of the third world but not completely absent in the developed world" (57). The *Koloko* fiction eloquently reiterates that societal tragedy is inevitable if leadership serves nothing more than mere consolidation of power, a position which Goran Hyden aptly puts this way:

> Through reform of the structural legacies inherited from the colonial power, as well as through mobilization of the masses,

politics was seen to serve national development. This conceptualization of politics, however, also served as an invitation for leadership to concentrate political power. Development became top-down affair, and politics increasingly an activity confined to a small clique of people. The later ran away with politics, so to speak, turning public matters into private and making a mockery of political accountability. (ix)

Children of Koloko begins with what an ideal society should look like. This is amply demonstrated in Yoyo's observation of how the ant community organize themselves. Yoyo imagines a system that is inclusive, no high ups and no low downs, they are all involved in the business of building the community from where they all eat:

> These creatures were great workaholics. Their home sands were neatly piled around the holes, mounting steadily. It's always a busy day after rains ...
> Soon I could find the workers busy doing the job, steadily, doggedly to salvage the remaining stock. They deposited, doggedly to salvage the remaining stock. ... others were scouting for alternative accommodation. I saw some of them wandering as if aimless, but purposeful. (3)

This system cuts a radical departure from the human community where some individuals are reduced to mere beggars of what is supposed to be their entitlements. The journey from Boko to Koloko is not only bumpy but horrible. The masses can not even work out modalities to free themselves from the crutches of misrule and corruption. For example Yoyo wryly states that "... no one really got to know why our land remained backward and undeveloped till the dawn of the new millennium. Only our leaders could tell us why" (20).

A keen observation of the anatomy of the socio-political structure of Koloko will no doubt confirm that the bane of African nations is the people. They are so concerned and content with squabbling for the crumb from the tables of rulers like Fathead and others, to the extent that they callously trump their political rights for something else. However, the rulers presume that the people exist to provide them with position. The tragedy of the oppressed is that they cannot see the truth that their position exists to free the sovereignty. For example Da Kata lavishes encomium on Fathead (Chief Ayadu) because she is deprived of her entitlements as citizen and given something less than her right which she begs for. Kata muses after she is offered a little drink, "I drank the wine he poured for me in a glass. That kind of wine has never passed my throat before" (24). As her state of health deteriorates she accosts the local council boss who should have put facilities in place to meet the needs of the sick. Fathead in his majestic sense gives her a few notes and she exclaims, yet again, about the Fathead's magnanimity and kind gesture for given her a little of what he has stolen from their commonwealth. But Yoyo teases: "The Chief is a generous man … He has done well, hasn't he?" (24).

The political structure of Koloko is fraught with numerous 'absences'. The absence of the electorate, absence of true democrats and politicians, absence of formidable political parties, absence of an outstanding opposition, absence of credible elections, absence of civility in governance and absence of due process. The Koloko ruling class is an exemplum of intellectual and moral deceit. The class is heavily hedonistic, that it does not know what its class interest is and their obligation to the electorate, their employers. Dogkiller and his like continue to sacrifice their nation at the altar of greed; they steal as much as they can, thereby pauperizing the society, making the gulf between the ruled and rulers widen with the passage of time. With Western 'progress' the ruling class has grown more callous, sentimental, and egocentric. For example, Dogkiller who has stolen so much money still amasses more property, while Fathead proudly stands at the verge of completing his M5 apartment, when those who voted them into office sustain themselves with subsistence farming, a system which hardly gives them enough to eat. The spate of fraudulence in Koloko reveals that corruption is deeply entrenched in the society because the leaders like Chief Ayadu (Fathead) and Dogomutun (Dogkiller) lead a life of chicanery. Tina's mother, Fathead's wife, decides to quit her marriage for her husband's lack of propriety. Fathead is "bringing three more women" (105) at the same time into his house and, funny enough, one of them is Tina's friend who is of her age.

This political configuration that concentrates power in the hands of a few people creates an oligarchy characterized by an absence of justice and rule of law. The conflict between individual and established authority in Koloko lies in the very heart of this problem. The Koloko judiciary systems and, its institution are there for the sole purpose of safeguarding the interests of the ruling class and hence work to confuse or coerce the people. Dickie's outrage over Buff's threat to tell on him for the chicken theft eloquently testifies to the above assertion:

> 'And you will pay two hundred for looting De Ndu's farm. Remember the law states whoever steals, and that include pears'. I reminded him.
> 'Such stupid laws' observed Buff.
> 'Much overkill for little mischief, while everyone including the Chief would readily commit worse crimes daily,' Dickie added. (37)

We are witnesses to a society trapped in a dilemma of conflicting values where the issues of duty, self-sacrifice and service to community remain pendulous. The incidents in the novel's fictional universe parallel the Nigerian political situation. The rulers when voted into office forget they are supposed to be representatives sort of to the electorate who gave them their mandates. The argument over the lamentation of the total neglect of Koloko eloquently testifies to the above contention:

> 'Maybe if we had a son in government'. I proposed
> 'It would have been a different story'.
> 'But we did,' countered Dickie. 'What about the Air Vice Marshall Keiba who was in the ruling council and Major General Bull? We had Rear Admiral Duckhead too.'
> Buff took over: 'General Ali Baba, Chief Idu, Engineer Fathead ... so many of them.' (19- 20)

If their aspirations were properly represented, there ought not to be complaint about marginalization. However, the rulers are unable to distinguish between representation, sacrificial leadership and the protection of their private interests. Fathead erects a gigantic structure in Koloko and on some occasions parts with a few notes and gags the people with the lavish parties he organizes. Representation or representativeness is not merely about inclusiveness, but about empowerment, and making the people have the necessities of life. The stories' argument is that the modern democracy hardly empowers, but it is the legitimization of disempowerment. Once the people are disempowered they are reduced to the status of sycophants and beggars.

Pathetically the Koloko rulers, like Nigerian leaders, lack knowledge of what constituency representation is. For example, the entire nation ought to be the constituency of the president of the country. Moreover, the electioneering formula dangerously moors on a zero-sum game; the syndrome of the winner takes all. A good example is Ribo Rice's attitude towards Koloko after the tribunal gave him victory. This parallels Chief Naiga's carting away pipes meant for Urua water scheme in Chinua Achebe's *A Man of the People*. There is a great deal of misreading of what democracy and representation are. Once the electorate fails to cast their votes for a particular candidate, and if such candidate eventually wins, he sees those who did not vote for him as his foes and (s)he will do everything within his/her powers to ensure such community never feel the impact of government.

In *Children of Koloko* the consequences of an inequitable distribution of resources are clearly enunciated, lending credence to Robert Young's opinion that "poverty and starvation… are often not the mark of an absolute lack of resources, but arise from a failure to distribute them equitably …" (35). Thus the luxurious and expensive cars and the prodigious building of the rulers eloquently testify to the fact that the economic debility of the people is informed by the exploitative inclination of the rulers and the doddery of the ruled. Ce aptly juxtaposes the wretched poverty of the ruled with the affluence of these opulent rulers.

The novelist also addresses ethnocentrism as the result of serious ethnic rivalry in Nigeria –a very ugly aspect of the polity which has left the federated units dangling in spite of Nigeria being labelled a federation. Dickie is unable to gain admission to college because of the quota system, a product of ethnicity which has bred what is characterized today as 'federal character'. Dickie becomes a victim of a national schema where ethnic politics is entrenched. Dickie's traits of psychopathic obsessive behaviour may also be karmic as Yoyo insinuates. But it is the economic and political drudgery of

Koloko that creates this melancholy, internalizes the pains of neglect and marginalization to regress into psychosis. The insensitivity of the rulers to the plight of the ruled turns out to be the source of Dickie's shattering perplexity. Although Dickie is not actually identified either as somebody from a minority or majority ethnic group, through this character the novelist demonstrates that a society anchored on the primacy of ethnicity could spell doom for the members of such society. The quota system in the narrative is undoubtedly a metaphor, which epitomizes the harsh and oppressive terrain that the Nigerian minorities must overcome in their match towards national integration. Says Gavin Williams:

> The politicians had made it quite clear that their looting of public resources could not be challenged within the frame work of electoral politics. Popular participation was limited to begging politicians to secure for individuals and communities a small slice of national cake (55).

Thus the people of Koloko continue to wobble in their abject state as they celebrate their rulers who are never accountable for their stewardship. With the passage of time, the harsh economic state of Koloko can only create individuals who are petty thieves like Yoyo and his friends and healthy beggars like Da Kata and Ade. It becomes imperative that for the African legal sovereignty to remain unambiguously sovereign, it has to make beggars out of the ruled. That way the masses will always be thankful for the crumb from the tables and any attempt at resistance will fail.

This attempt to resist depraved leadership in Koloko is offered by Goodman. However his idea for a revolution is without ideological mass. It fails not because he lost the election, but because the people to champion the cause of their liberation have no faith in the ideology of an egalitarian society. Moreover a revolution cannot survive because the leader of the revolution wants to run for election at the embryonic or introductory stage of his revolution. Goodman is trapped in a matrix of clichés and rhetorical outrage while his political evangelism is sequestered in hollow, stale and inconsequential slogans. In addressing a group of young in a rural society, rather than cite copious examples of what they can easily see and comprehend, for example, how he will change the agricultural system and make them produce beyond the substance level when voted into power, he takes them on an excursion of how developed nations winch themselves from the backwaters of underdevelopment to technological productivity. Goodman symbolises neither the elite of society who neither understand society's yearnings and aspirations nor the superstructure of power politics. Ce seems to demonstrate that vaulting into a revolution is not the panacea to Africa's economic and political problems. Understanding the people is what matters. An acute knowledge of the people will therefore lead to the formulation of a people oriented ideology which will gradually grow and give the people a sense of belonging. This will in turn give them the acuity to discern their rights and help them rupture the political tension in Africa. Goodman's followers hardly understand the basis of the revolution, hence one of the youths insists he will vote for his "brother in the liberal party" (77).

The palm wine 'revolution' of Goodman is thus proof that the people of Koloko need no sermons of revolution to rupture the socio-political tension. Their lives, characterized by abject poverty, the lack of basic amenities in the community, the plight of retirees like Foreman Obeku, Yoyo's father, and Goodman, would have been enough to spur them to action, yet they are content with the squalor of the slums they regard as home. Because of this contentment with their own myopia, the rulers regularly invest in short-term distractions, like Fathead's lavish parties, instead of long-term projects that will better the lives of the people. Through Goodman's "revolution", the novel tactically addresses one of post colonial nations' biggest political issues –the issue of electioneering.

Elections are mainly conducted by (s)election as the electorate are not given a free hand to make their choice among the aspirants. It is voting without choice. If the defining characteristic of democracy is choice, this is lacking in African democratic systems for reasons which include multiple registrations, hoarding of voters cards, under aged registration, impersonation, forgery, block recruitment of agents, poor training of ad-hoc staff, late delivery of electoral materials, inflation of accredited numbers, thuggery and falsification of results by the election commissions. The African electioneering process could best be described as selection or better still allocation of position. This allocation of position is flawlessly conducted today by Nigeria's Independent National Electoral Commission of Nigeria (INEC). In "Bards and Tyrants" Chin Ce had contended quite rightly that "Nigeria today is ... a democracy where leaders or winners are selected from political drawing tables and executive lists" (16). The emergence of the president of the youth vanguard in *Children of Koloko* becomes his fictionalization of the realities of the Nigerian electioneering process. Goodman's revolution is grounded and founded on nothing of substance, hence it crashes. Goodman's political suicide lies in not understanding the political matrix of his society.

Chin Ce's idea is that what the people need most importantly are moral rearmament and socio-political re-conscientization which will, in turn, give them the right political direction. Tanure Ojaide captures this functionality

106

when he avers that "literature has to draw attention to the increasing gap between the haves and the have nots. Literature has become a weapon against the denial of basic human rights" (125). Thus Ce's narrative may pass the test of utilitarian function of African literature in the second half of the twentieth century which hinges heavily on the exposure of political corruption and authoritarianism but it fails to indicate an alternative from the mired present. Although a military regime truncates the civilian government, this change is supposed to be a quantum leap but nothing actually has changed in the fortunes of the people. They continue to wobble as the society remains in what Paul Becket and Crawford Young describe as "permanent transition" (4). The society is in a flux –the process of being but never arriving. Moral values have been eroded from the society by values which in turn send the society crashing from its delicate idyllic temper. The tragedy of Koloko becomes whole as the younger generation loses focus at a tender age and their conducts demonstrate that their motive for wanting power is not far from that of the present crop of rulers. Thus they lack the vision and conviction to redeem their society from the precipice of collapse. Yoyo's rhetorical question which his colleagues responded to with a sudden revulsion becomes emblematic of this tragedy:

> 'Now to you children of our father and mothers,' I asked, "If the Khaki boys went back to barracks today, who among us wouldn't want to make more money and buy a ministerial seat like the Chief of Koloko did?' (120)

Not surprisingly too, the narrator-protagonist is very inconsistent and his character is as ambivalent as Koloko itself. He may be just like Ayi Kwei Armah's protagonist in

The Beautyful One Are Yet Not Born, who ambles all through the novel. He does nothing pragmatic to change his situation and that of his society but continues to sustain himself in a permanent state of inconsistency and passivity. At the least, he could be better described as an observer or crippled commentator –just like the people of Koloko. Thus the novel captures varied issues in his story, the most strident being the debility of the people and the welfare of the state without proffering a solution to the crisis. Perhaps the life of the ants in the first chapter could be a parable. Maybe, the author intends to recommend an alternative through the organisational structure of the ant kingdom –which is idyllic by all standards. As Jo Okome opines:

> Art has always served to articulate the people's responses to the changing phases of society by trying to shape perceptions of events and in the process creating a model towards change. As a result, the artist is always socially conscious and realistic, he is always alive to the realities and forces operating in his/her society. (95)

The crises in the African continent have been evinced in almost every sphere of human endeavour –politically, economically, socially, and culturally. And as Ambrose Kom passionately laments:

> The multidimensional failure of our institutions: phantom states in search of an undiscoverable democracy, an extrovert economy which is almost entirely controlled by corrupt networks; a disjointed society whose essential services –schools, public health, personal safety in particular– seem irremediably compromised; young people who are crippled, left to themselves in a world without any ethics. (3)

This abysmal portraiture of the execrable political state of contemporary Africa is by no means contentious. A critical appraisal of recent African literature reveals more horrid pictures. *Children of Koloko* dismally showcases the problems of post independence Nigeria in particular and Africa at large. But there are no strategies in the resolution of the dire economic crisis that continues to reduce Africa, which Bill Ashcroft subtly puts as the "conflict between a dominant discourse and a local reality" (1). Koloko seems void and empty yet, the emptiness does not suggest vacuity, strictly because it is peopled by individuals who sustain themselves at the borderline of docility and a perpetual state of inertia. They have succumbed to the monstrous dictates of capitalistic doctrines and exploitative mechanism of a handful of narcissistic and egocentric individuals who privilege themselves at the core of the juicy economy of state. Since the political sovereignty is unable to purge itself of the overdose of barbiturates laced with juicy doctrines of hope offered them by their legal sovereignty, it appears the ruled may continue to support themselves with the beggarly crutches of mass poverty. If this trend continues unchecked, African societies, no doubt will remain economically and socially asymmetrical.

We may conclude that Chin Ce's *Children of Koloko*, palpably suffused with metaphors and symbols of thieves, exploiters and bad leaders, aptly demonstrates that greed and lust have been part of Africa's history and experience. It is a work of great satirical depth where even naming is also a metaphor. The etymology of the names of some characters evokes a sense of sarcasm. Through this sarcasm, Ce attains narrative sagacity which is devoid of any form of ironic intentionality. For example Chief Dogkiller's true name is Dogomutun, a Hausa word which means a tall individual. However nothing is tall about the physical or moral qualities of this leader. Goodman on the other hand has good intentions for the people of Koloko, but he never gets the opportunity to exhibit himself as an earnest leader hence after his loss at the polls he begins to sustain himself at the border of existential solitude suggesting that good people like him, with the will for sacrificial service, hardly find their way into the power towers of Africa.

With *Children of Koloko* Chin Ce graphically demonstrates that not until the low downs recognize their limitations, which lie in their scatteredness, will the rulers discontinue confining them in the marginal borders of poverty. The victory of the oppressed will only come when they realize that power belongs to them, only then will they overcome their vertigo and rightly distinguish between their rights and privileges.

Chapter Six

Memory and Trauma

S.A.Agbor

HERE we focus on the relationship between literature and memory and, thus, address a theme that over the last two decades has become one of the central issues in literary and cultural studies. Memory and literature intersect in many different ways. Literature is one of the media that plays a crucial role in the process of representing and constructing both individual and collective memories. Throughout literary history, literary texts have engaged in a discussion of the implications, the problems, and the purposes of remembering (uni-giessen.de). Literature, moreover, participates in the processes of shaping collective memories and of subversively undermining culturally dominant memories by establishing counter-memories, which seek to consider, for example, gender-conscious or ethnic perspectives on past events. One of the recurring themes as far as literary representations of memories are concerned is the complex interaction between memories and identities. The intimate relationship between literature and memory is particularly obvious in genres such as autobiography, biography, or fictional biography.

The Anglophone problem is a historical reality in Cameroon and has had a profound influence on the literary imagination of many Anglophone writers from Bole Butake to

Epie Ngome to Bate Besong, to Charles Alobwed'Epie and John Nkengasong amongst others. Modern Cameroon is made up of Anglophones and Francophones because the nation was colonized by the British and French. The Anglophones in Cameroon are a minority, constituting about one-fifth of the population and occupying less than one-tenth of the national territory. Alobwed 'Epie states that "in Cameroon usage, the term is used to designate the opposite of Francophone on the one hand and, on the other, to designate people native to the S.W (Southwest) and N.W (Northwest) provinces" (49). Although fact is mixed with fiction, Nkengasong's text educates and allows the reader to participate in the (re)creation and (re)interpretation of events and processes that form identity crisis and alienation in a nation. Moreover, the manner in which Nkengasong manipulates characterization, storytelling, and imagination to enact memory is enriching. Across the Mongolo is relevant in the information it coveys and functions as historical data and as an avenue through which nationhood and bilingualism in Cameroon are conceived.

Now we shall aim to explore various facets of the intimate and complex relationship between literature and memory from different vantage points in Nkengasong's *Across the Mongolo*. We hope to show that the subject of the Anglophone problem has indeed inspired a range of reflections on the notion of memory, trauma, and history. It intersects with Nkengasong's creative springboard. His creative imagination is influenced by a multiplicity of social, cultural, political, and economic trends of the Cameroon nation. The argument here begins with this recognition. Alienation, we contend, is as central to *Across the Mongolo* as neocolonization. Secondly, through his creative imagination Nkengasong reveals the tension and predicament of a minority in the nation. It is in this wise that we refer to the

Anglophone Cameroonian as the "other other". The primary importance of *Across the Mongolo* is exemplified in its vivid representation of the anguish and victimization of the "other other" in a struggle against alienation and a search for identity, particularly when citizens are forced to choose between personal autonomy and identity.

Of relevance to this study are the questions: in what way is Across the Mongolo a cultural and political memory? How does this literary representation of socio-cultural and political realities act as an individual and collective memory of pertinent issues related to identity and trauma in the Cameroonian society? What are the implications of this memory and what knowledge does the reader get from this novel? Our hypothesis is that *Across the Mongolo* is a representation of memories and conflicting identity in the Cameroonian society.

In this story, the past is omnipresent for the novel begins at the end. The novelist manipulates flashback to tell us the cause of the protagonist's trauma. *Across the Mongolo* tells the story of Ngwe's struggle to acquire an education. The story is told across the eighteen hills of Attah that Ngwe "had lost his head" (1). The Fon, the Royal father of the land summons "his troh-ndii, the executive council of the land" (2) and orders them to tell the youths to go and bring Ngwe back to this land (3). The youths set off and before the next market day, Ngwe is brought back looking "different from the proud brown earth of the land from which he rose" (3). He looks "dazed and dumb to the world, deaf to the world, blind to the world, absent from the world which looked at him with sorrow in the grief of the moment" (3). "Instead of achieving academic excellence, a logical stepping to his aspirations, Ngwe meets physical, emotional, intellectual and psychological frustration, which push him inexorably into madness and near tragedy"

(Ngongkum 8). Alabi, the diviner works on Ngwe but there is no change. Only one man in the land, Aloh-Mbong who is their master, can cure Ngwe. Ngwe is taken to Aloh-Mbong's shrine where for one week he can only eat and sleep. Aloh-Mbong performs another divination and blows air into Ngwe's nostrils and ears saying, "Ngwe, son of the hills… Purge out the awful things that you have done to men so I can make you sleep in peace, so that I can clear those shadows that men have trapped your inside with"(6). Aloh-Mbong further tells him:

> Speak, my son! Send out the bad vapour from your belly, with the power of Fuandem, clear the rust of time that has eaten into your mind so that you can sleep. Speak, my son! (6)

This is where the process of memory begins in the novel. Ngwe "heaved a terrible sigh as if he heard a sharp pain inside him, like one in a dazzled trance, like one in a perpetual dream … and narrated the story of his life" (6). In "The Generation of Memory: Reflections on the "Memory Boom" in Contemporary Historical Studies", Jay Winter states:

> The biochemistry of traumatic memory is now a field of active research, and various pathways have been identified that help us distinguish between memory as recall and memory as re-enactment. There is now a biochemistry of traumatic memories, memories that are first buried and then involuntarily released when triggered by certain external stimuli. The world of neurology has had its own memory boom, which in turn has helped establish the scientific character and credentials of the notion of "trauma". (par. 51)

Ngwe's memory is first stifled because of the painful experiences he undergoes. Aloh-Mbong recognizes that except this memory of the past is "recalled" and "reenacted" the protagonist will not be cleansed and healed. For Kerwin Lee

Klein the evocation of memory becomes a kind of "cultural religiosity," a "re-enchantment" of our sense of the past (par.63). Aloh-Mbong feels that if Ngwe resurrects the past enough, it will purge him of his madness. This past is recollected through memory and remembering. Ngwe seems to finally have a calling from the past, from his memory and his inner voice cries:

> I have never done anyone any harm, not even Monsieur Abeso. I am a university student, Constitutional law. No, History. Oh, gods of my ancestors! Oh, Shirila! Darling Shirila! What else did you want? What is the meaning of this world? Have they no consciences, Babajoro and his acolytes? He cannot live long....Why did he dread the Young Anglophone Movement?... I will tell the world everything;...I will tell you just how I travelled to that far away land, to Besaadi, to the University of Besaadi where I went to read law to become Babajoro of Kamangola.(7)

In Ngwe's narrative, the theme of memory is re-enacted when he says"... I will tell the world everything...I will tell you just how I travelled to that far away land, to Besaadi...(7). In remembering these stories, he exposes the atrocities which lead to his traumatic state. In this manner, he relates to the reader how his metamorphosis takes place and what leads to his present predicament. All these are embedded in Ngwe's memory. All of his dignity and person is taken away; all except the memory of his victimization and alienation. By the third chapter of the novel Ngwe screams:

> See!...they are coming. Babajoro's men are coming to arrest me. I shall flee to the village. Babajoro's men are coming to slaughter me. I was the leader of the Young Anglophone Movement. We wanted our rights as full citizens of the republic of Kamangola. Please let me flee. Don't hold me down! Please, allow me to escape. They will slaughter me. Babajoro's men, they will kill me. (27)

The memory of the past results in some kind of schizophrenia, defined as a state of split personality (Olaogun 70). Modupe O. Olaogun in her article entitled "Irony and Schizophrenia in Bessie Head's *Maru*" states:

> Schizophrenia evokes an image of a cleavage of mental functions. In its strictly medical sense, Schizophrenia...refers to a mental illness manifested by a splitting of the capacity for thought. Schizophrenia is; a term applied to a form of psychosis in which there is a cleavage of the mental function, associated with the assumption by the affected person of a second personality. (70)

As a schizophrenic, Ngwe experiences certain disorders manifested in his thinking and exteriorized in his behaviour as exemplified in the quotation from the text above. It is an example of visual hallucination. The protagonist manifests emotional crisis and a splitting of the capacity for thought as a result of the socio-cultural and political trauma he undergoes. This also leads to identity problems. Thus we are also made aware of the sometimes overpowering nature of memory. This memory is transitory; it reverberates in the secret inner being of Ngwe. The protagonist's memory is made up of scattered and different traumatic experiences that are dependent on the unexpected and uncontrollable events of his life. He is influenced by the vagaries of recollections and that are shaped by the interplay of remembering and forgetting a very painful and traumatizing experience as a student in the University of Besaadi located in "the capital city of the Federated United Republic of Kamangola" (58-9). Besaadi stands for Yaounde the capital city of Cameroon while Kamangola represents the Cameroon nation. The title of the novel signifies the bridge that separates West Cameroon from East Cameroon. The author manipulates symbolic imagery to represent the dichotomy between the two cultures. Geographically the Anglophones are located within the area west of the River Mungo. Ngwe leaves his village to travel to the "University of Besaadi" (Yaoundé) where he goes to study law to become Babajoro of Besaaadi. Ngwe recounts that immediately as the "vast expanse of plantations ended a huge arched steel structure appeared 'before us' (36). This is the Mongo Bridge and Ngwe further recounts: "it seemed that it chained two worlds together and below was a deep dark abyss" (36). The man sitting in front of him says: "The River Mongolo. It is the Great River, the boundary between the English colony of Kama and the French colony of Ngola, the two federated states that gave birth to the Federal Republic of Kamangolo" (37). Richard A. Goodridge in "Activities of Political Organisations: Southern Cameroons, 1945-61" states that:

> in recent times, public debates about the Anglophone position in Cameroon has been dominated by what is described as the 'Anglophone problem' which, according to Konings and Nyamnjoh, poses a major challenge to the efforts of the post-colonial Cameroon state to forge national reconstruction, unity and integration. (13)

The Anglophone problem caused a lot of debate in the 1990s. Nkengasong attempts to look at this problem from the eyes of a student. An Anglophone is broadly speaking a person who speaks English particularly where English is not the only language spoken. This definition includes a bilingual Cameroonian whose official language is French (186). But in the context of this text and in the Cameroonian society, Anglophones are "people who speak English and are native to the S.W and N.W province" (Alobwed' Epie 57). Cameroon initially had three colonial masters. Walter Gam Nkwi emphasizes that "as far as Cameroon is concerned, the territory and its indigenes have experienced three colonial masters and, ipso facto three distinct foreign languages" (186). The first colonial master was Germany, which annexed this territory in July 1884. Germany was defeated in 1916 and the "territory was partitioned between France and Britain" (186). Following the Mandate of the League of Nations, Britain was "authorized to administer her part of Cameroon as an integral part of Nigeria" (186). This part was known as the British Southern Cameroon, which finally gained independence by reunifying with the Republic of Cameroon which was, and spoke, predominantly French. This is evident in the novel where Ngwe further recounts: "it seemed that it chained two worlds together and below was a deep dark abyss (36). The man sitting in front of him says: "The River Mongolo. It is the Great River, the boundary between the English colony of Kama and the French colony of Ngola, the two federated states that gave birth to the Federal Republic of Kamangolo" (37). The 'River Mongolo' is the Mungo River that separates the South West Province -one of the two Anglophone provinces- from the Littoral Province- a Francophone province in Cameroon.

The novel concentrates on the alienation and deprivation experienced by the Anglophone Cameroonian under a majority Francophone rule. Alobwed 'Epie insists that "today, Anglophone Cameroonians can look back in anger, or pleasure, and tell us how they felt being second-class citizens in their supposed area of jurisdiction" (54). Nkengasong recounts the journey to the Mungo River. The car that brings Ngwe swerves to the right side of the road and stops abruptly with a screech (37). He hears "harsh blasts of whistles- Pirrrr! Pirrrr! Pirrrr! Pirrrr!" [and] a voice shouting with "such violent authority" 'Piece! Identité! Impot!' Three gendarmes wearing red berets scampered about the window," (38). Anglophones dread the Gendarmes who often victimize them.

At the Scolarite (Admissions office) Ngwe describes the way he is treated when he goes to register as a student. The man at the table collects his documents and looks through them with a sour expression. "Relevez de notes, monsieur!" he barks. Ngwe does not understand what he says and asks in English "'What Sir?'" The man sighs and flings the documents at him saying: "Les Anglos aiment toujours les annouilles. Sort, monsieur. Suivant" (60). Ngwe goes on his knees pleading and becomes a source of mockery and ridicule to the excited students who jeer at him "Pauvre Anglo! Anglo for Kromba. Tu ne pouvez pas rester chez vous à Kromba, Anglo? "(60). The Francophone students see him as an alien. Emmanuel Fru Doh emphasizes that "...because of his minority status, the Anglophone is a second-class citizen who is watched, always suspected" (77). Anglophone students have to spend money translating notes from French to English. All their lecturers are 99% French (64) except Dr. Amboh "who in spite of his rich academic background in legal matters was never given a main course to teach" (64). Dr. Amboh explains to some of the Anglophone students that this under utilization of his expertise is "government policy to eliminate the Anglophone culture in the country using the university as one of its weapons, we had no choice but to give in to complete assimilation into the Francophone culture" (64). The puzzling thing is that Francophone lecturers are not obliged to teach in English: "None of them seemed to have an idea in English: they stressed that all answers had to be in French and not English" (64). Once Ngwe asks a question in class in English, the lecture hall breaks "into a tremor of booing and jeering "Anglo! Anglofou! Anglobete!" (64). Francophone students throw papers and assorted objects from every direction on him.

Thus the Anglophone is marginalized and the "other other" in a country he calls his nation. Nkengasong incorporates the sense that the margin which is the lot of Anglophone Cameroonians under the current regime is also a physical, intellectual and psychological space with its own dynamics, tensions and contradictions. In this state of 'otherness', Anglophone students live a life of want, disillusionment, and sexual discrimination from their Francophone brothers. As a result they find themselves helpless. Ngwe laments:

> I was the Anglo, the pariah, the slave that had no voice in the high and decent life across the Great River. At all cost, I had to learn the language of my masters and talk to them and write my examination in the language. ...Why, had I to ask a question in English when my masters, my assimilationist masters, forced me to speak their own language? (65)

Any Anglophone student who answers questions in English definitely would fail the exams. Nwolefeck consoles Ngwe saying:

> You cannot blame any Anglophone who does not succeed here. It is the system. Not that we do not work hard. We do not know French and we do not answer our questions during Exams in French. How do you expect to succeed? (100)

Surprisingly, Anglophones in posts of responsibilities treat their brothers in the same way. Ngwe and Nwolefeck go to the ministry of Education to apply for a scholarship. The chief of Service in charge of scholarship Mr. Kwenti is an Anglophone. Rather than offer them assistance, he shouts and orders them to leave his office, speaking in French (101). For

Ngwe, this is one of series of traumatizing incidents. He soliloquizes:

> My brother, Kwenti, disowned me because I spoke the language of the pariah and I was going to contaminate him with the vapours of the English Language. My brother Kwenti who traveled like me across the Great River from Kama disowned me in the middle of the stream. These thoughts ached my mind... I had no appetite, unable to reconcile myself with the struggle for survival... (102)

The impact of his alienation and rejection by his own brother is unacceptable to his sensitivity. These double standards in the manner Anglophones are mistreated lead to identity crisis. Mickey Pearlman in the "Introduction" to Canadian Women Writing Fiction writes that "the concept of identity, always and everywhere in flux, was shaped by ethnicity, race, culture, habit and even social policy" (4). Pearlman argues further that "identity evolves not only from place and site, from birth and perception, but in reaction to someone else's perception of you" (5).The perception the Anglophone has concerning his identity and belongingness is that he is the second class citizen in this nation –Cameroon. Consequently he feels marginalized and alienated.

According to Nkwi "the Anglophone problem is essentially the coming together of two cultures -the Anglo Saxon and the Gaullic" (187).What grows obvious is that in spite of the marriage between the East and the West, the two are not together or united. In this novel, victimization and brutalization lead to psychological, emotional, and physical disorder as exemplified in the protagonist's dilemma. Brutalization is to be feared because it forces Anglophones "to submit to other standards" of nationhood. Victimization then is the instrument used to enforce those standards. At the Resto (student cafeteria) disorder is the order of the day. Ngwe emphasizes:

> Disorder was the intellectual principle that guided the lives of undergraduates, the lives of future leaders of the nation. Disorder, it was clear, was the order of the day in Besaadi. There was no alternative. Therefore I came to obey the dictates of violence and disorder without getting close to it, even without seeking it as a means of survival. (77-78)

Writing about the strike in the mother state university allows Nkengasong to show the centrality of alienation, oppression and violence to the narrative of class oppression. Eunice Ngoumkum in her review of *Across the Mongolo* praises "the novelist's grasp of historical events" as "profound and through his character, Ngwe, he lashes out at the ironies and cruelties of history" (8). The students have waited for the list and disbursement of their scholarships. "There were rumours that the ministry had already disbursed the money but the university authorities were playing tricks to deprive the students of their meager sums" (102).Tension mounts and some students in the faculty of law plan a violent demonstration to disrupt lectures. Angry students move from one lecture hall to another carrying "hammers, long nails and a coffin" (103). The Resto (restaurant) is attacked. The cooks and the administrative staff of the Resto are caught and thrashed and the Resto is looted. Cars are smashed or set on fire. The rioting students assemble in front of the chancellery chanting songs of misery and suffering, insisting and wanting "Dr. Mballape, the chancellor for life of the university, dead or alive" (104). Dr. Mballape comes out and says nothing. Suddenly panic seizes the atmosphere as furious military men "tore into the mob from all directions, whipping, fighting, and throwing tear gas on the students" (104). The students flee into the bushes and the following day the students regroup carrying a coffin to the chancellery. The soldiers advance on the surging students as if in a state of war. The soldiers charge "spraying very offensive tear gas, hitting and beating the students ruthlessly, arresting and flogging them" (107). Unfortunately, Ngwe is caught while looking for a safe place to hide. He recounts: "Hard boots cleared my feet from behind and I went with my whole body, face first, and crashed on the grainy tarmac" (107). The police man smashes him on his chest and he falls with his back, head first. He bleeds profusely and still manages to plead his innocence. Once the police realize he is Anglophone they speak with so much hatred "'C'est une Anglo, meme. La, tu est morte!'...Un Anglo, chef!'...Un de leader de la greve qui fuite" (108). Although he insists on his innocence, they fall on him, hit his jaws "with the butts of their rifles, with baton sticks..." smashing "his toes with their heavy boots" cursing "Anglofou, esclave, idiot, salaud, Anglo!" (108). They arrest and take him to the Cinquieme {the fifth district police station). The other police officers stare at him furiously saying "'mon dieu! Un Anglo? Il est finit! They said" (109). The issue here is that an Anglo, "the other" is caught. His crime is that he is an Anglophone. While in the dungeon, a traumatized Ngwe cries: "What offence have I committed against man, against God? Why did they maltreat an innocent child that much? Why was I made to suffer assault and brutality without cause? Why was I born an Anglophone?"(110). Ngwe pleads his innocence crying: "..I know nothing sir..." and yet, he is tortured beyond measure. The commissioner shouts "Parlez en francais, idiot! Est-ce-que je comprends ton patois la?"(113). The commissioner brands him dangerous and further calls for the balancoire. The policemen drag him towards "an object that looked like a swing". They fasten his wrists and ankles to it "and switched

123

on the current". Ngwe says "the machine swung me out of life" (114). The split the protagonist experiences between his aspirations, fears and dreams and his consciousness is revealing. Ngwe says "That night I could not say whether I was alive or dead. My mind was blurred with dull grey images, incomprehensible images; flickers of my mother busy with household chores and sighing; my father's spirit standing by her side…" (114).

The memory of violence is manipulated by Nkengasong as a means to critically re-examine the past and its mistakes. It is this violence that traumatizes Ngwe with the nightmare he experiences and the eventual state of schizophrenia he manifests. Violence is centered mainly on the Anglophone students and Ngwe, depicts in vivid terms the abuse and torture they experience. The author confronts us with the utter destruction and dislocation of society where postcolonial violence can be seen as only a continuation of colonial violence and practices of domination and power. In this wise Odile Cadinave's insistence that "violence works in two main ways: as a pretext to look at the past and at traditional values and to revisit history and as an illustration of current times and a contextualized violence" (64) is quite apt. Cadinave cites other examples of writers who have written such texts:

> works by Jean-Roger Essomba, Gaston-Paul Effa, and Ludovic Obiang [show how] the child narrative and the presence of violence serve as a point of departure to step back and reflect on history, on the rapport between memory and history, and how history is shaped by the collective.(61)

In this novel Ngwe's (Nkengasong's ego) process of rememorizing is to revisit the history of the strike action of the 1980s and the manner in which Anglophone students are marginalized. This memory of this strike articulates the dilemma of students. This strike have political undertone and refers to a historical period in Cameroonian higher education. Nkengasong draws on the past as it is recorded in a range of documents -real and imaginary- to create a narrative that derives its historical interest from the factual and memory, that most porous and unreliable of recipients of knowledge. One of the most interesting aspects of Nkengasong's novel is this weaving of the political with the personal, in order to make a statement about a historical reality and show how history is manipulated as a springboard for creative imagination. It is in this imprint of life as it is found in memory that Ngwe -the ego of Nkengasong- recounts. This is his experience of university life. These are his university memories.

Conclusion

Across the Mongolo opens up new vistas to citizenship and nationhood. The theme of "remembering" is central to the protagonist's healing and purging because it is through this medium that he reconstructs his history, and in the process he comes to terms with his reality and supposedly comes out of his psychological trauma. His memory becomes a collective memory bank from which we gain an insight into the strike and predicaments of Cameroonian students of the eighties. Nkengasong's narrative pieces together his experience as a student, reinterpreting it in such a way as to transcend the gap between personal and the collective. Nkengasong writes this novel from a desire to depict the complexities of the Anglophone in Cameroon, the challenges of nationhood. The only way that the character could transcend his predicament is to purge himself by remembering the past in order to come to terms with his situation. Through this process of remembering and retelling his story, Aloh-Mbong makes Ngwe come to terms with the root of his trauma. For Ngwe the incidents of the past lead to his trauma and only by coming to terms with his story can he overcome his temporal schizophrenic state of being.

Chapter Seven

Ethno-lingual Issues

K.M. Gqibitole

Introduction

SOUTH African radio drama has been historically ethnic-specific while not realistically reflecting the society in a holistic sense. In modern South Africa, questions of multiculturalism and multilingualism are of extreme importance. In other words, different language groups not only learn to co-exist; they also learn to share their cultures.

In spite of its popularity, research shows that radio drama has been generally neglected in mainstream scholarships (Traber 56). This neglect should not be construed to mean that radio has no impact in the society. Since its introduction in the 1920s, radio has played a pivotal role in the socio-political sphere of South Africa. For African language radio stations, their traditional role seems to have been to promote the apartheid policy of 'separate development' of languages. As one of the rules on radio drama on the Xhosa language station states, 'Good Xhosa should be used –avoid slang and abusive language and English and Afrikaans', (Umhlobo Wenene 1986). By adopting only a specific African language, dramas do not correctly reflect the multiracialism/multi-tribalism of the South African society. By confining drama to one language only the dramas miss the opportunity to talk to the nation as a whole, and not only to a select group.

There are many factors that hinder experimentation with multiple voices in South African radio dramas. First is the unwillingness of African radio stations to 'experiment' with multilingualism. Since programming is targeted to a specific audience, South African language radio stations may not see the need to change their format. This unwillingness may be fuelled by the fact that radio dramas still attract a sizeable audience compared to other programs. Secondly, playwrights may not have the necessary expertise to deal with multilingualism. Thirdly, a majority of audiences may not appreciate the use of other languages in the dramas. Finally, minority groups who had been marginalized in the past often view multilingualism as a means to undermine their languages. Such challenges though can be overcome if focus is on nation-building and not on 'separate development' that was engineered by the apartheid regimes.

An attempt will be made in this final chapter to place radio drama within literary and cultural studies. In other words, radio drama can be made to serve as an object of study just like any other literary genre. Since radio drama contains qualities accessible to the broader society, such information should not be locked up in the archives as is the practice at present. Its utilitarian value in reconciling divergent language groups is also of paramount cultural merit.

Background and Evolution of SA Radio Drama

The involvement of the Broederbond in the running of the South African Broadcasting Corporation from around the late 1930's (Ryan 39) had never been underestimated. The power politics between the Afrikaners and the English in the period preceding World War II were, to an extent, waged on the airwaves. By the time the Afrikaners ascended to power in 1948, decision makers and politicians in general had come to realize the pervasiveness of radio and its power. It was within that culture of entitlement that the separatist policy in broadcasting was developed and entrenched by the subsequent Afrikaner regimes.

It is not accidental then that the introduction of radio was delayed for Africans. Even when it was finally gradually introduced from 1941 (Gunner 216), radio texts were 'doctored' to serve the audiences according to ethnic and racial lines. As Hendy points out, many Africans who owned radio sets resorted to listening to foreign radio stations from countries such as Mozambique because of these policies, (222).

Notwithstanding the debilitating system of apartheid that had engulfed the operations at the South African Broadcasting Corporation (SABC), radio, as Traber notes, became very popular --especially among the poor. Poor communities were not only politically and socially sidelined; they were also unable to access other sources of information. As a result of this they solely rely on radio for entertainment and education. It is within this premise that the Afrikaners established the homeland system with each homeland having 'its' radio station. Based on this, different communities have traveled through time without intermixing except in a master/servant relationship.

Consequently, different races and language groups are strangers and at times even hostile to one other. Owing to the stereotypes that have developed over decades, different race groups speak across each other instead of speaking to each other.

Radio texts can ably take the challenge of reconciling the different groups but at the moment they seem to fail. For instance, many radio dramas try to paint a purist view of the black communities. In other words they present black culture as largely rural and as such 'uncontaminated' by other cultures and languages. As Makhosana correctly points out,

> the literary history of radio drama broadcast from the seventies up to the present reveals that the themes that are tackled most include traditional values compared to those of modern life, the corruption of urban life compared to rural life, historical themes and problems in marriage. (7)

Due to this inflexible approach, radio dramas are predictably tribal, discriminatory and unrealistic. This unfortunately rules out the participation in the plays by other language groups. As a result, the dramas create a falsified community that does not come into contact with other language groups.

In the play Kubhetele Kwalapha Ehlathini ("It is better here in the forest") by R. G. Swartz, the main character, Nzimeni, is a forester who ensures that endangered trees are not chopped down. He is a hard worker who is not liked by his fellow workers for his dedication to his work. At the back of his mind though, Nzimeni tries to raise money so that he can pay lobola (bride-price) for his intended wife, Thandiwe. Up until he manages to raise enough amount, the play 'seems' to be about a young man who is not only dedicated to his work but also determined to marry Thandiwe.

This is typical of many plays but in most cases the young man would go to the mines to raise the money -a replica of the migrant labor system. Mines necessarily introduced young men to city life -a life they should not be exposed to. Instead of following the trend of many African playwrights, Swartz chooses the forest instead of the mines. In almost all plays that toe the apartheid line, the city is depicted as a dangerous place for black people, while the rural is peaceful and safe. In this case the forest Nzimeni works in symbolizes the rural area - a safe haven for him and his kind.

To make this point clear, Swartz takes Nzimeni to town (King William's Town) to buy some clothes for himself and his future wife. While in town he is mugged and the money is stolen. In anguish he cries, 'Yintlalo yasedolophini le? Kungcono kwasehlathini!' ('Is this town life? It is better in the forest!') Just as in Alan Paton's Cry the Beloved Country, the city is corruptible and dangerous to the black man. To a large extent, R.G. Swartz is a typical white who wishes black people only as laborers and not as neighbors. It is not surprising that there is neither a white person in the play nor the police to rescue Nzimeni. The only whites (Nzimeni's employers) are only referred to.

Ultimately, Swartz's Kubhetele Kwalapha Ehlathini demonstrates a lack of understanding of black people. The play is not only insulting; it is stereotyped and informed by the policy of apartheid.

However radio stations such as Ukhozi FM and Umhlobo Wenene FM (formerly Radio Zulu and Radio Xhosa respectively) still enjoy a bigger chunk of the audience, to a large extent they still serve specific language groups (i.e. Zulus and Xhosas). Since drama is an entrenched activity among many South African communities, it follows that the genre can be used to reunite different language and race groups. By creating realistic social situation radio drama can go a long way in making different language and race groups understand each other because radio drama would mirror the society and lead to the healing of the wounds of the past through mutual understanding.

The question of multilingualism and multiculturalism therefore remains pertinent in the study and development of South African radio drama. Cultural exchanges that take place on the field of play and other cultural gatherings go a long way in bridging the gaps in the country, although these are inadequate and sometimes contrived. Labels such as 'the rainbow nation' perhaps do play a role. However, such activities do not penetrate the psyche of individuals who, in the seclusion of their homes, are (perhaps unintentionally) bombarded by messages of segregation. Radio dramas can address these deep seated prejudices.

Crossroads

Modern South Africa is at the cross roads in realizing the true meaning of inter-racialism and multilingualism which can only take place if and when everyone knows and has access to the others' languages and cultures.

For some enthusiastic audience, the love for radio drama may transcend cultural or racial boundaries. At one point a radio drama fan found himself far away from home at a time his favorite drama played. Finding himself in a coloured area he had to ask from them to let him listen to the play. He writes:

> I was caught up sixteen miles from home at that time. I dropped into the home of coloured people and requested them to allow me to listen to the Bantu program the particular play acted. We were welcome - after the play we thanked them and off we drove, (Umhlobo Wenene radio archives 1986).

The reality of the South African society is that it is a community made up of different race and language groups. The post independence period in the country has made South Africa not only a boiling pot of different race and language groups but also of different nationalities. The relaxing of border controls between South Africa and her neighbors, the relative peace and prosperity enjoyed in the country, our role in African Renaissance as well as our accommodative external policy play a big role in attracting different people from across the world into the country. Radio drama should reflect this development in order to teach locals about other nations. Xenophobic attacks that take place in places such as Cape Town and elsewhere can be greatly reduced if such programs are encouraged on national radio stations.

Traditionally, radio drama is believed to target the 'illiterate', rural listeners. This myth is worsened by the fact that a large number of poor, black listeners resides in the rural areas. As a result of the reality of the economic situation, many people cannot afford other sources of information and entertainment except radio. This is a myth that needs to be dispelled. This has had a tendency of isolating rural people, as many of the plays still do.

As a microcosm of the society, radio dramas tend to replicate the reality on the ground. Since South Africa is a multilingual and multicultural society, all the eleven languages demand to be equally promoted. It is in this spirit that radio drama could handle the issues of multiculturalism and inter-racialism; by forging unity through multilingualism. It is, therefore, important that playwrights recognize the potential of radio drama in this regard. There might be no need, for instance, to cast a Xhosa speaking character for a role that should be played by either a Zulu speaker, as is the case in

Mandla Myeko's play, Nangona Intliziyo Ithatha Ibeka, or a white speaker, as is the case in A.C. Jordan's Ingqumbo Yeminyanya. In the former drama the igqirha (witch doctor) Gonondo speaks Zulu but is played by a Xhosa speaking character, while in the latter the white bishop is also played by a Xhosa speaking character. In Jordan's play there is no attempt to 'make' the bishop speak English or 'broken' Xhosa for that matter. Unlike in the TV version of the play, the bishop is a white man who tries hard to speak Xhosa. This is the lead that radio drama should follow if the dramas are to be realistic to the listener.

Voices from other language groups are conspicuous by their absence in Xhosa radio drama, rendering the plays not only stereotyped but also isolationist. In the play USomagqabi by Kheswa, for instance, an opportunity to hear other voices is lost. The play is about the origin and the relationship between the Nguni people during their 'great trek' from North Africa to south east Africa. They include Xhosa, Zulu, Swati, Phuti, and Ndebele. None of these voices are brought to the fore except Xhosa. Even the warriors they fight with on their 'trek' are just referred to -they never speak. While it is true that playwrights are bound by the rules that govern the dramas, it is equally true that a chance to reconcile the different language groups is missed in the process. During the dark days of apartheid such limitations would be understandable, but in the post independence era they are intolerable.

New Challenges and Trends

To appropriate a title from Mongane Wally Serote's novel: 'To every birth its blood', if it wants to serve a wider spectrum of audiences, radio drama has to negotiate through many obstacles and challenges. At the top of the list is the willingness and capability of playwrights to venture into the unknown. Embracing different language groups calls upon the playwrights to be multi-skilled and understand the intricacies of race relations in the country. As Hau Mbatha concedes, 'audiences are creatures of habit' and as such any change in the format and focus of the dramas may affect listenership. Any changes that may be effected may result in the station losing audiences. However, as with the change of the names of the stations illustrated, with time the audiences would pay their patronage to the station. The other challenge concerns minority languages. If and when other languages are given a space in their slots, they would infringe upon the airtime of these formerly neglected languages. One of the priorities of African radio stations is to nurture and promote specific languages. With the 'intrusion' of other languages this goal may not be realized.

The popularity of radio drama can be manipulated in various interesting ways to benefit the entire society. Firstly, radio drama can be used to encourage reading since some radio dramas are adapted to novels. This is mostly true of Zulu radio drama. Sibiya is of the opinion that some prominent Zulu novelists cut their teeth in radio drama writing and actually popularized their books by initially writing them as dramas (26-27). Novelists such as DBZ Ntuli, Michael T. Mkhize, Vusumuzi Bhengu, Emelda Mankayi Damane, Ncamisile Makhambeni, Mlindeli Gcumisa are just some of those who used the radio space as a springboard to writing novels. In the Xhosa language radio the reverse is true because it is novels which are mainly adapted to radio drama. A.C. Jordan's Ingqumbo Yeminyanya (The wrath of ancestors), S.E.K. Mqhayi's Ityala Lamawele (The lawsuit of the twins) are just two examples. The idea is that, after listening to the dramas the listeners may want (and can be encouraged) to read the book. They may lead to an increased engagement with the text and promote discussion around the issues raised.

Secondly, the novels that are adapted to drama may be used to forge reconciliation among different groups. Since members of other language groups may not be able to access a novel written in Xhosa, a conscious and deliberate inclusion of other voices could be made where necessary. Adaptation and modification of some texts to radio drama for reconciliation purposes could be engaged in. For example, the adaptation and translation of Shakespeare's Macbeth by Welcome Msomi to UMabatha in the 1970s was a huge success. The play did not only revive interest in Macbeth but it also showcased Zulu language and culture; creating new audiences in the process. In a sense, radio drama can be written and adapted to suit modern African social conditions. The possibilities are unlimited in this regard.

Radio and TV may compete for the same audience. While this is inevitable, the two mediums can work hand in glove in drama. Both have inherent handicaps which can be addressed if they work together. Radio is a blind medium which solely relies on the voice. Promoting multilingualism through radio drama may be an arduous task both for playwrights and producers. Trying to change the format of the dramas may not only be a challenge to playwrights but may also prove costly to the station. Unfortunately, unlike TV, subtitling is impossible on radio and as such the audience will have to do with the cacophony of languages. While such would be reflective of the world 'out there', this may alienate a number of audiences. As an audio-visual medium, TV can come to the rescue of radio. The adaptation of radio drama, and the introduction of subtitles in the process, can go a long way in addressing multilingualism. Television dramas such as Mhuvango (SABC 3) and Isidingo -the Need (SABC 3) are just two examples of programs that seek to address the questions of multilingualism and multiculturalism. By taking on board radio drama, television would be addressing its need to increase the local content when it comes to dramas. The adaptation of great radio dramas such as Nongona Intliziyo Ithatha Ibeka, Yiyekeni Inkwenkwe Izonwabele and Buzani Kubawo, would make excellent viewing. Above that, it would give audiences from across the language spectrum a better understanding of their country.

Conclusion

Radio drama can be used to promote multiculturalism and multilingualism in the society. As an educational tool, radio drama can play a huge role in supplementing learning material in schools. South Africa is a culturally diverse society and radio dramas can play a crucial role in cultural exchange, thereby deepening understanding between different race groups. By encouraging and promoting multilingualism, radio drama can serve as a catalyst to bring together different language groups. On the whole, the dramas not only raise awareness about different cultures, traditions and languages, they also critique the socio/economic life of the community. In a sense, dramas give the listeners an opportunity to reflect on their lifestyles and prejudices with a view to changing imbedded stereotypes while at the same time they educate them on a variety of pertinent issues.

The role of television in ensuring that radio plays do not only reach a wider audience, but also truly reflect the country's demographics should be encouraged. Moreover, scholarships on radio drama should be encouraged, especially in higher institutions. It is when radio drama is formally studied at universities that the genre will gain its rightful status as a powerful instrument of cultural production.

Notes and Bibliography

Chapter One
Shades of Utter(ing) Silences

Notes

1.Basic law of communication was introduced by psychologist and linguist Paul Watzlawick in the 1960s.

2.In the sense of imitating, copying the line of arguments; a counter-argumentation in the form of a one to one reflection.

3.Or to use Hélène Cixous's words who writes from the French context: to "give [.. them] back [... their] bodily territories which have been kept under seal" (351).

4.For easy reference, the following abbreviation is used: PV.

5.For easy reference, the following abbreviation is used: UT.

6.Also cf. Samuelson, "A River in my Mouth," 15-24.

7.Vera's works suggest a reading which establishes an affinity between a woman's body, the land and the nation. Whereas Nehanda displays the conquering of land and her subsequent killing with imperialist domination, "Independence Day" leads a discourse around men metaphorically equating the taking over of land with their sexual exploitation of women's bodies, and civil war fighters raping and torturing women's bodies as a metaphor for their war in shifting political power relations in The Stone Virgins, Without a Name and Under the Tongue, as discussed in Meg Samuelson's essay "Re-membering the Body," "can be read on the allegorical level as using rape to signify [the psychological scars of] colonial invasions into the land occupied by the Shona, and the [anticipated] post-independence betrayal of Zimbabweans by a national government [in which women are the main losers]" (93).

And as Samuelson argues in an earlier essay "Reclaiming the Body": "The rape from within the family in Under the Tongue issues searing attack on the betrayal of post-independence governance and shatters the familial trope of nation" (2). Vera opposes national discourses that claim to purify and restore the abused female body/land; the symbol of the Nation 'Mother Africa' is not re-establish. To back up her study, Samuelson cites Gayatri C. Spivak's résumé: "for the subaltern, and especially the subaltern woman, 'Empire' and 'Nation' are interchangeable names, however hard it might be for us to imagine it" ("Reclaiming the Body" 2).

8. The unspeakable refers to a taboo whereas the unsayable only indicates the inability to be said (Mills and Smith 2)9.Darkness is associated with horror, destruction, and taboo; the moon, similar to the metaphor water, as a place of rebirth and closely connected with women.

10. Zhiza's anxiety about grandmother's death may suggest her dread of the impossibility of finding a new language to describe the unspeakable.

11. As Rosi Braidotti asserts in her essay "Mothers, Monsters, and Machines," "[a]dequate representations of female experience [...] cannot easily be fitted within the parameters of phallogocentric language" (60).

12. As to this repeated reference cf. UT 5, 12, 20, 21, 30, 41, 53, 54, 61. According to Adrienne Rich, 'speaking silence' can be a mode of healing and may form the beginning of a narrative, of finding a voice for one's experience (qtd. in Hoogestraat 27).

Works Cited

Andreas, Neshani. *The Purple Violet of Oshaantu*. Oxford: Heinemann, 2001.

Baumann, Hermann. *Schöpfung und Urzeit des Menschen im Mythus der Afrikanischen* Völker. Berlin: Dietrich Reimer, 1964.

Braidotti, Rosi. [Ed.] "Mothers, Monsters, and Machines." *Writing on the Body: Female Embodiment and Feminist Theory*. Katie Conboy et al. New York: Columbia UP, 1997.

Case, Dianne. *Toasted Penis and Cheese*. Wynberg: Kwagga, 1999.

Cixous, Hélène. "The Laugh of the Medusa." *Feminisms: An Anthology of Literary Theory and Criticism*. Ed. Robyn R. Warhol, and Diane Price Herndl. New Brunswick: Rutgers UP, 1997.

Duras, Marguerite. *La pluie d'été*. Paris: POL, 1990.

Eppel, John. "Suffering and Speaking Out." *The Zimbabwean Review 3.3* (1997):

Gray, Stephen. "The Unsayable Word." *Mail & Guardian* Mar. 1997.

Head, Bessie. "Life." *The Collector of Treasures and other Botswana Village Tales*. Ed. Bessie Head. Oxford: Heinemann, 1992.

— — —. "The Collector of Treasures." *The Collector of Treasures and other Botswana Village Tales.* Ed. Bessie Head. Oxford: Heinemann, 1992.

— — —. *Maru.* Oxford: Heinemann, 2000.

Hoogestraat, Jane. "'Unnameable by Choice': Multivalent Silences in Adrienne Rich's Time's Power." *Violence, Silence, and Anger: Women's Writing as Transgression.* Ed. Deirdre Lashgari. London: UP of Virginia, 1995.

Leibowitz, Stacey, et al. "Child Rape: Extending the Therapeutic Intervention to Include the Mother-Child Dyad." *Southern African Journal of Psychology 29.3* 1999

Mills, Alice, and Jeremy Smith. *Utter Silence: Voicing the Unspeakable.* New York: Peter Lang, 2001.

Phiri, Virginia. *Desperate.* Harare: Virginia Phiri, 2002.

Samuelson, Meg. "'Grandmother Says We Choose Words, Not Silence': Trauma, Memory and Voice in the Writings of Yvonne Vera." MA thesis. U of Leeds, 1999.

— — —. "Reclaiming the Body: A Memory for Healing in Yvonne Vera's Writing." A Symposium on Zimbabwean Literature: Scanning Our Future, Reading Our Past. U of Zimbabwe, Harare. 1-12 Jan. 2001.

— — —. "A River in My Mouth: Writing the Voice in Under the Tongue." *Sign and Taboo: Perspectives on the Poetic Fiction of Yvonne Vera.* Ed. Robert Muponde and Mandivavarira Maodzwa-Taruvinga. Harare: Weaver Press, 2002.

— — —. "Re-membering the Body: Rape and Recovery in Without a Name and Under the Tongue." *Sign and Taboo: Perspectives on the Poetic Fiction of Yvonne Vera.* Ed. Robert Muponde and Mandivavarira Maodzwa-Taruvinga. Harare: Weaver Press, 2002.

Shostak, Marjorie. *Nisa: The Life and Words of a !Kung Woman.* Cambridge, Massachusetts: Harvard UP, 2001.

Signori, Lisa F. *The Feminization of Surrealism: The Road to Surreal Silence in Selected Works of Marguerite Duras.* New York: Peter Lang, 2001.

Stone, Elena. *Rising from Deep Places: Women's Lives and the Ecology of Voice and Silence.* New York: Peter Lang, 2002.

Stories of Courage Told by Women. Women's Shelter Project 2000. Gaborone: Lightbooks, 2001.

Trinh, T. Minh-ha. "Not You/Like You: Postcolonial Women and the Interlocking Questions of Identity and Difference." *Dangerous Liaisons:*

Gender, Nation & Postcolonial Perspectives. Anne McClintock, et al. London, Minneapolis: U of Minnesota P, 1997.

Veit-Wild, Flora. "Gebrochene Körper: Körperwahrnehmungen in der kolonialen und afrikanischen Literatur." *Fremde Körper: Zur Konstruktion des Anderen in europäischen Diskursen.* Kerstin Gernig. Ed. Berlin: dahlem UP, 2001. 337-355.

Vera, Yvonne. *Nehanda.* Harare: Baobab Books, 1993.

—— — . *Without a Name.* Harare: Baobab Books, 1994.

—— — . *Under the Tongue.* Harare: Baobab Books, 1997.

—— — . *The Stone Virgins.* Harare: Weaver Press, 2002.

Vigne, Randolph, [Ed.] *A Gesture of Belonging: Letters from Bessie Head, 1965-1979.* London: SA Writers, 1991.

Watzlawick, Paul. *Wie wirklich ist die Wirklichkeit? Wahn, Täuschung, Verstehen.* München, Zürich: Piper, 1998.

Wicomb, Zoë. *David's Story.* Cape Town: Kwela Books, 2000.

Chapter Two
Counter-Discourse and Reworking the Canon

Note

1.See: Ngugi, wa Thiong'o. "Europhonism, Universities and the Magic Fountain: The Future of African Literature and Scholarship." In Research in African Literatures". 31.1, (2000): 2

2.Schipper, Minneke. Imaginning Insiders: Africa and the Question of Belonging. (New York: Cassell, 1999): 34.

3.See: Bill Ashcroft, et al, The Empire Writes Back: Theory and Practice in Postcolonial Literatures. (New York: Routledge, 1989): 63, and Homi Bhabha, The Location of Culture (London: Routledge, 1994): 31.

Works Cited

Achebe, Chinua. *Things Fall Apart.* London: Heinemann, 1958.

– – – . "The Novelist as Teacher." *New Statesman,* 1965, 160-170.

– – –. *Hopes and Impediments: Selected Essays, 1965-1987.* London Heinemann, 1988.

Ashcroft, B, G Griffiths and H. Tiffin. *The Empire Writes Back: Theory and Practice in Postcolonial Literatures.* New York: Routledge, 1989.

– – –. *The Postcolonial Studies Reader.* London: Routledge and Kegan Paul, 1995.

Attridge, Derek. "Oppressive Silence: J.M Coetzee Foe and the Politics of the Canon." *Decolonizing the Tradition: New View of Twentieth-Century "British" Literary Canons.* Karen Lawrence Ed. Urbana: University of Illinois Press, 1992,212-238.

Attwell, David. *J.M Coetzee South Africa and the Politics of Writing.* California: University of California Press, 1993.

Bhabha, Homi. "The Commitment to Theory." *New Formations, Vol. 5,*1988, 1-19.

– – –. *The Location of Culture.* London: Routledge, 1994.

Blyden, Edward Wilmot. *Christianity, Islam and the Negro Race.* Chesapeake, New York: ECA, 1990.

Cary, Joyce. *Mister Johnson.* New York: Harper, 1951.

Chinweizu, Onwuchekwa Jemie and Ihechukwu Madubuike. *Toward the Decolonization of African Litearture.* Enugu: Fourth Dimension, 1980.

Coetzee, J.M (1986). *Foe.* London: Secker and Warburg, 1986.

– – –. "Two Interviews by Tony Morphet 1983 and 1987". *Triquarterly. No 62,* 1987, 454-464.

Defoe, Daniel (1719/1994). *Robinson Crusoe.* London: Penguin, 1719/1994.

Emenyonu, N. Ernest. "Nationalism and the Creative Talent." *Goatskin Bags and Wisdom New Critical Perspectives on African Literature.* Ed. Emenyonu (ed.) Trenton, New Jersey : Africa World Press, 2000, 377-386.

– – –. "Telling Our Story: A Keynote Address at the 15th International Conference on African Literature and the English, Language (ICALEL)", at the University of Calabar, Nigeria, May 7-11.2002.

Fanon, Frantz. *Black Skin, White Masks.* New York: Grove Press, 1967.

– – –. *The Wretched of the Earth.* Trans. Constance, Farrington. Harmondsworth, Middlesex: Penguin, 1970.

Foucault, Michel. *Power/ Knowledge: Selected Interviews and Other Writings, 1972-1977.* Ed. Colin Gordon. Brighton: Harvester, 1980.

Gallagher, Susan. *A Story of South Africa: J.M Coetzee's Fiction in Context.* London: Harvard University Press, 1991.

Jameson, Fredric. "Third-World Literature in the Era of Multinational Capitalism." *Social Text.Vol. 15,* 1986,65-88.

JanMohammed, Abdul R. Manichean Aesthetics: *The Politics of Literature in Colonial Africa.* Amherst: U of Massachusetts P, 1983.

143

Korang, Kwaku Larbi. "An Allegory of Rereading: Post-Colonialism, Resistance and J.M Coetzee's Foe." *Critical Essays on J.M Coetzee.* Ed. Sue Kossew. New York: G.K Hall and Co., 1998, 180-197.

Kossew, Sue. "Introduction." *Critical Essays on J.M Coetzee.* Ed. Sue Kossew. New York: G.K Hall and Co, 1998, 1-17.

– – –. "The Politics of Shame and Redemption in J.M Coetzee's Disgrace. *Research in African Literatures, 34.2,* 2003,155-162.

Lomba, A. *Colonialism/ Post-Colonialism.* London: Routledge and Kegan Paul, 1998.

McVeagh, John. "The Blasted Race of Old Cham, Daniel Defoe and the African." *Ibadan Studies in English, 1. 2,* 1969,85-109.

Milner, Andrew and Jeff Browitt. *Contemporary Cultural Theory -An Introduction.* London: Routledge, 1991.

Nagy-Zekmi, Silvia. "Tradition and Transgression in the Novels of Assia Djebar and Aicha Lemsine." *Research in African Literatures, 33. 3,* 2002, 1-13.

Ngugi, wa Thiong'o. *Homecoming.* London: Heinemann, 1972.

– – –. "Europhonism, Universities and the Magic Fountain: The Future of African Literature and Scholarship." *Research in African Literatures. 31. 1,* 2000. 1-22.

Osundare, Niyi. *African Literature and the Crisis of Post-Structuralist Theorizing.* Ibadan: Options Books, 1993.

Palmer, Eustace. *Studies on the English Novel.* Ibadan: African University Press, 1986.

Penner, Dick. *Countries of the Mind: The Fiction of J.M Coetzee.* Westport, Connecticut: Greenwood, 1989.

Preckshot, Judith. "An Historical Obsession: Counternarration in CoRachid Mimouni's Tombeza." *Research in Africa Literatures, 34.2,* 2003,155-162.

Rodney, Walter. *How Europe Underdeveloped Africa.* London: Boyle-L'ouverture Publishers, 1972.

Rushdie, Salman. "The Empire Writes Back with Vengeance." London Times, (July 1982), 334-45.

Said, Edward W. *Orientalism.* New York: Pantheon Books, 1978.

– – –. *The World, the Text and the Critic.* Cambridge: Harvard UP, 1983,31-53.

— — —. "Intellectuals in the Post-Colonial World," *Salmagundi. 70. 71,* 1986,44-66.

– – –."Representing the Colonized: Anthropology's Interlocuters." *Critical Inquiry, 15.3,* 1989,205-225.

– – –. *Culture and Imperialism.* London: Chatto and Windus, 1993.

Schipper, Minneke. *Imagining Insiders: Africa and the Question of Belonging.* New York: Cassell, 1999.

Spivak, Gayatri Chakravorty . "Theory in the Margin: Coetzee's Foe Reading Defoe's Crusoe/ Roxana." *English in Africa, 17.2,* 1990, 1-23.

– – –."Can the Subaltern Speak?" *Colonial and Post-Colonial Theory.* Eds. Patrick Williams and Laura Chrisman. New York: Columbia UP, 1994, 66-111.

Tiffin, Helen. "Post-Colonial Literatures and Counter-Discourse." *KUNAPIPI, 9. 3,* 1987,17-34.

Valdiz, Moses M. "Caliban and his Precursors: The Politics of Literary History and the Third World." *Theoretical Issues in Literary History.* Ed. David Perkins. Cambridge: Harvard UP, 1991, 206-226.

Viola, André. "J.M Coetzee: Romancieur Sud Africaine." *Journal of Commonwealth Literature.* L' Harmattan, Vol. 6, 1999,69-78.

Walder, Dennis. *Post-Colonial Literatures in English History, Language, Theory.* Oxford: Blackwell, 1998.

Zukogi, Maikudi Abubakar. "The Post-Colonial Text as Counter-Discourse: A Re-reading of Armah's Two Thousand Seasons." A Paper Presented at the 15th International Conference of African Literature and the English Language (ICALEL), University of Calabar, Nigeria. May 7-11,2002.

Chapter Three
Tegonni: an African Antigone

Note

1.Lori Chamberlain remarks on the field of translation studies and its reliance on male-centered metaphors to describe the function of translation, and attempts "to examine what is at stake for gender in the representation of translation: the struggle for authority and the politics of originality informing this struggle" (Chamberlain 314-15).

Works Cited

Aidoo, Ama Ata. *The Dilemma of a Ghost.* Modern African Drama. Ed. Biodun Jeyifo. New York: Norton, 2002. 242-275.

Azodo, Uzoamka Ada. "The Dilemma of a Ghost: Literature and Power of Myth." *Emerging Perspectives on Ama Ata Aidoo*. Ed. Ada Uzoamka Azodo and Gay Wilentz. Trenton, NJ: Africa World Press, 1999. 213-240.

Bartlett, Juluette F. Promoting Empowerment for Woman: Women between Modernity and Tradition in the Works of Tess Onwueme. Diss. University of Houston, May 2002.

Bhabha, Homi K. "The Third Space: Interview with Homi K. Bhabha." *Identity: Community, Culture, Difference*. Ed. Jonathan Rutherford. London; Lawrence & Wishcart, 1990. 207-221.

Brown, Lloyd W. *Women Writers in Black Africa*. Westport, Connecticut: Greenwood Press, 1981.

Chamberlain, Lori. "Gender and the Metaphorics of Translation." *The Translation Studies Reader*. Ed. Lawrence Venuti. London: Routledge, 2000. 315-329.

Dunton, Chris. *Make Man Talk True: Nigerian Drama in English since 1970*. London: Hans Zell, 1992.

Elder, Arlene A. "Ama Ata Aidoo: The Development of a Woman's Voice." *Emerging Perspectives on Ama Ata Aidoo*. Ed. Ada Uzoamka Azodo and Gay Wilentz. Trenton, NJ: Africa World Press, 1999. 157-169.

Eveirthoms, Mabel. *Female Empowerment and Dramatic Creativity in Nigeria*. Ibadan, Nigeria: Caltop Publications, 2002.

Gourdine, Angeletta KM. *The Difference Place Makes: Gender, Sexuality and Diaspora Identity*. Columbus: Ohio State University Press, 2002.

– – –. "Slavery in the Diaspora Consciousness: Ama Ata Aidoo's Conversations." *Emerging Perspectives on Ama Ata Aidoo*. Ed. Ada Uzoamka Azodo and Gay Wilentz. Trenton, NJ:Africa World Press, 1999. 27-44.

Gyimah, Miriam C. "The Quest for Power and Manhood: Three (Neo) Colonial Male Characters of Ama Ata Aidoo." *Journal of African Literature and Culture. 1.3* (2006).

Lakoff, George and Mark Johnson. *Metaphors We Live By*. Chicago: UCP, 2003.

Odamtten, Vincent. *The Art of Ama Ata Aidoo: Polylectics and Readings Against Neocolonialism*. Gainesville, Florida: University Press of Florida, 1994.

Onwueme, Osonye Tess. *Legacies*. Ibadan: Heinemann Nigeria, 1989.

– – – . *The Missing Face*. San Francisco: African Heritage Press, 2002.

146

Rushdie, Salman. *Imaginary Homelands: Essays and Criticism 1981-1991.*
London: Granta, 1991.

Trivedi,   Harish.   "Translating   Culture   vs.   Cultural   Translation."
www.91stmeridian.org. May 2005 <http://www.uiowa.edu/
~iwp/91st/may2005/index.html.>

Uko, Iniobong *I. Gender and Identity in the Works of Osonye Tess Onwueme.*
Trenton, NJ: Africa World Press, 2004.

Chapter Four
Poetics of the Diaspora

Notes

1.Bessora also does this in 53 cm by inserting historically incongruous
figures and at times changing their gender or crucial markers.

2.See: Aimé Césaire, Suzanne Césaire et René Ménil. Tropiques 1941-
1945. (Paris: Jean Michel Place, 1978).

3.Since the 17th century, France has constructed its history based on
notions of racial and linguistic purity, excluding all histories of immigration.
It is not until very recently (within the last decade) that France has begun to
recognize its immigrant past. This "coming to terms" with an alternative
history is exemplified in the establishment of a new history of immigration in
Paris as well as a re-working of the museum of primitive arts exemplified in
the establishment of a new museum of immigrant history in Paris, la Cité
nationale de l'histoire de l'immigration <www.histoire-immigration.fr> and a
new   museum   of   "arts   primitifs,"   the   Musée   du   quai   Branly
<www.quaibranly.fr>.

4.Here, I am referring to the use of the preposition "de" at the beginning of
each chapter. i.e. "De l'altérité dans la règne gymnasale," 53 cm, 11.

5.In opposition to the Exposition Coloniale in Paris (1931) the surrealists
organized a counter Exposition Coloniale whose aim was to decenter common
beliefs regarding colonial practice at the time. Drawing on the personal
collections of his friends, Aragon brought together sculptures from Africa,
Oceania, and the Americas, so that the people could see the artwork of these
countries on their own terms, away from the atmosphere of imperialism that
pervaded the "Musée des colonies" at Vincennes.

6.See: James Clifford. "On Ethnographic Surrealism." Comparative
Studies in Society and History, Vol. 23, No. 4 (1981): 539-564).

147

7.Here, movement is present in two forms. The first is by moving (in the gym) to shape her body into the pure state expected by the nation. The second is the continual movement to and from the official government offices in search of the cartes. This is connected to the notion of quest or journey in the surrealist context.

8.Her word plays with "ca't," " cat' " and " act'" could be discussed in terms of the surrealist practice of automatic writing .

9.See: Michel Foucault, Surveiller et punir (Paris : Gallimard, 1975).

10.See : Ousmane Sembene, Le Mandat (Paris : Présence africaine, 1966) and Jean-Michel Adiaffi, La carte d'identité (Paris: Haiter, 1980).

Works Cited

Adamowicz, Elza. "Ethnology, Ethnographic Film and Surrealism." *Anthropology Today, Vol. 9, No. 1* (1993).

Adiaffi, Jean-Marie. *La carte d'identité*. Paris: Hatier, 1980.

Bessora, *53cm*. Paris: Serpent à plumes, 1999.

– – –. "The Milka Cow." *From Africa: New Francophone Stories*. Ed. Adele King. Lincoln: University of Nebraska Press, 2004.

Breton, André. *L'amour fou*. Paris: Gallimard, 1937.

– – –. *Manifestes du surréalisme*. Paris: Gallimard, 1962.

Célérier, Patricia-Pia. "Bessora : de la 'gautologie' contre l'impérité." *Présence Francophone, No. 58* (2002): 73-84.

Césaire, Aimé, Suzanne Césaire and René Ménil. *Tropiques 1941-1945*. Paris: Jean Michel Place, 1978.

Clifford, James. "On Ethnographic Surrealism." *Comparative Studies in Society and History, Vol. 23, No. 4* (1981): 539-564.

Dayal, Samir. "Diaspora and Double Consciousness," *The Journal of the Midwest Modern Language Association, Vol. 29, No. 1*, Spring 1996.

Foster, Hal. "Convulsive Identity." *October. Vol. 57* (1991): 18-54.

Foucault, Michel. *Surveiller et punir*. Paris: Gallimard, 1975.

Lionnet, Françoise. *Postcolonial Representations: Women, Literature, Identity*. Ithaca: Cornell University Press, 1995.

Richardson, Michael. "Surrealism Faced with Cultural Difference." *Cosmopolitan Modernisms*. Ed. Kobena Mercer. Boston: MIT Press, 2005.

Sembene, Ousmane. *Le Mandat*. Paris: Présence africaine, 1965.

Sharpley-Whiting, T. Denean. *Negritude Women*. Minneapolis: University of Minnesota Press, 2002.

Chapter Five
The Rhetoric of Despair

Works Cited

Amuta, Chidi. *The Theory of African Literature*. London: Zed, 1989.

Ashcroft, Bill. "Legitimate Post-Colonial Kowledge". *Mots Pluriels. No. 14* June 2000. http://www.arts.uwa.edu.au/motspluriels /mp:1400akfr:html.

Beckett, Paul and Crawford, Young. (ed). *Dilemma of Democracy in Nigeria*. Rochester: U of Rochester Press, 1997.

Ce, Chin. *Children of Koloko*. Enugu: Handel Books Ltd, 2001.

– – –. "Bards and Tyrants: Literature, Leadership and Citizenship Issues of Modern Nigeria (An African Writer's Travelogue)". *The African Literary Journal B5*. IRCALC, 2005. 3- 24.

Chukwuma, Helen. *Accents in the African Novel*. Lagos: Pearl Publishers, 2003.

Franco, Jean. "The Nation as Imagined Community." *The New Historicism*. Ed. Aram Veeser. New York: Routledge, 1989. 204 12.

Hyden, Goran, and Michael Bratton. *Governance and Politics in Africa*. Boulder: Rienner, 1992.

Khamis, Said. "Classicism in Shaaban Robert's Utopian Novel Kusadikika". *Research in African Literatures Vol. 32, No. 1*. Ed. Abiola Irele, 2001. 47 -65.

Kom, Ambrose. "Knowledge and Legitimation" Mots Pluriels. No. 14 June 2000. <http//www.arts/uwa.edu.au /motspmp1400akfr.html>.

Kubayanda, Josaphat. "Dictatorship, Oppression and the New Realism". *Research in African Literatures. 21, 2*, 1990. 5 11.

McGee, Patrick. "Texts between Worlds: African Fictions as Political Allegory". *Decolonizing Traditions: Views of Twentieth-Century "British" Literary Canon*. Ed. Karen Lawrence. Urbana: U of Illinois P. 1992. 239 60.

Ojaide Tanure. *Delta Blues & Home Songs*. Ibadan: Kraft Books, 1997.

– – –. *Poetic Imagination in Black Africa*. Durham: Carolina Academic Press, 1996.

Okome, Jo. "Protest and Praxis: Revolutionary Ethos in Tanure Ojaide's The Blood of Peace and Other Poems." *Writing the Homeland: The Poetry and Politics of Tanure Ojaide.* Ed. Onookome Okome. Bayreuth: Bayreuth University, 2002. 83 96.

Okunoye, Oyeniyi. "Exploration in New Nigerian Poetry." *Writing the Homeland: The Poetry and Politics of Tanure Ojaide.* Ed. Onookome Okome. Bayreuth: Bayreuth University, 2002. 19 30.

Williams, Garm. "Nigeria: The Neo-Colonial Political Economy." *Political Economy of Africa.* Ed. Dennis L. Cohen and John Daniel. London: Longman, 1981. 45 66.

Chapter Six
Memory and Trauma

Works Cited

Cazenave, Odile. "Writing the Child, Youth, and Violence into the Francophone Novel from Sub-Saharan Africa: The Impact of Age and Gender." *Research in African Literatures 36.2* (2005): 59-71.

Doh, Emmanuel Fru. "Anglophone Cameroon Literature: Is there any Such Thing?." *Anglophone Cameroon Writing.* Eds. Lyonga Nalova, Eckhard Breitinger, and Bole Butake. Bayreuth: Bayreuth African Studies, 30. WEKA No.1, 1993.76-83.

Epie 'Alobwede. "The Concept of Anglophone Literature." *Anglophone Cameroon Writing.* Eds. Lyonga Nalova, Eckhard Breitinger, and Bole Butake. Bayreuth: Bayreuth African Studies 30 WEKA No.1, 1993. 49-58.

Goodridge, A. Richards. "Activities of Political Organisations: Southern Cameroons, 1945-61." *Cameroon from a Federated to a Unitary State 1961-1972.* Ed. Victor Ngoh. Limbe: Design House, 2004.13-47.

Klein, Kerwin Lee. "On the Emergence of Memory in Historical Discourse." *Representations 69* (Winter 2000): 130- 136.

Ngongkum, Eunice. "John Nkengasong's Across the Mongolo." *Cameroon Post. No.0637,* Monday January 31st, 2005:8.

- - -."Dream and Reality in John Nkemngong Nkengasong's Across the Mongolo." A paper presented at a book launch (British Council, Yaoundé) 9 February, 2005.

Nkengasong, John Nkemngong. *Across the Mongolo.* Ibadan: Spectrum books, 2005.

Nkwi, Gam Walter. "The Anglophone Problem." *Cameroon from a Federated to a Unitary State 1961-1972.* Ed.Victor Ngoh . Limbe: Design House, 2004.185-209.

Olaogun, Modupe O. "Irony and Schizophrenia in Bessie Head's Maru." *Research in African Literatures.Vol.25.No.4.* Eds. Irele Abiola et al. Ohio: Indiana UP, 1994.69-85.

Pearlman, Mickey. "Introduction." *Canadian Women Writing Fiction.* Jackson: UP of Mississippi1993.3-11.

Winter, Jay. "The Generation of Memory: Reflections on the "Memory Boom." Contemporary Historical Studies. GHI Bulletin 27 Winter. June, 2005 <http://www.ghi-dc.org/bulletin27F00/b27 Winter fn.html#26>

Chapter Seven
Ethno-lingual Issues

Works Cited

Copland, D.B. *In Township Tonight.* London: Longman Press. 1985.

Dickinson, R. *Approaches to Audiences.* London: Arnold. 1998.

Ellena, J. S. and D.C. Whiteney. *Audience Making.* London: Sage. 1994.

Fardon, R and G. Furniss. *African Broadcasting Cultures.* Oxford: James Currey. 2000.

Goffman, E. *Forms of Talk.* Oxford: Basil Blackwell. 1981

Gunner, L. 'Resistant Medium: The Voices of Zulu Radio Drama in the 1970s.' *Theatre Research International. 27* (2002a): 259- 274.

– – –.'Zulu Radio Drama'. *Senses of Culture: South African Cultural Studies.* Eds. S. Nutall and C. A Michael. Oxford: Oxford University Press, 2000.

Hall, S. W. 'Encoding/Decoding.' Culture, Media, Language: *Working Papers in Cultural Studies.* Eds. S. Hall et al. London: Hutchinson, 1980.

Hendy, D. *Radio in the Global Age.* Cambridge: Polity Press. 2000.

Jordan, A. C. *Ingqumbo Yeminyanya 1976.* Radio Play. Cassette. Umhlobo Wenene FM, SABC 1976.

Kheswa USomagqabi 1986. Radio Play. Cassette. Umhlobo Wenene FM 1986.

Kirschke, L. *Broadcasting Genocide: Censorship, Propaganda and State-Sponsored Violence in Rwanda 1990-1994.* London: Article 19. 1996.

Modleski, T. *Loving with a Vengeance: Mass-Produced Fantasies for Women.* New Yolk: Methuen. 1982.

Potholm, C.P. *Southern Africa in Perspective: Essays in Regional Politics.* New Yolk: Free Press. 1972.

Ryan, G.C. *Public Service Broadcasting in South Africa: An Analysis of the SABC Fulfillment of a Public Service Mandate.* Masters Thesis, University of Natal. 2000.

Satyo, N.P. 'The Art and Craft of Sound Effects in Two Radio IsiXhosa Dramas.' *South African Journal of Languages. 21*(2001a): 176-185.

– – –.'The Woman as a Character in D.T. Mtywaku Xhosa Drama, Ufeziwe okanye Inkohlakalo'. *South African Journal of African Languages. 21*(2001b): 6 -8.

Satyo, N.P. and Jadezweni, M.W. 'The portrayal of Character through Dialogue in Saule's Drama.' *African Journal of Languages. 23* (2003): 1-10.

Saule, N. Amaciko: *Imidlalo Endimanye Yeradio.* Arcadia: Bard Press. 1988.

Sibiya, D. Postulating Audiences in isiZulu Radio Drama: Narration, Characterization and Theme in Mlaba's uNdlebekazizwa. A Paper read at the University of Birmingham, United Kingdom September, 2002.

Swartz, S. G. *Kubhetele Kwalapha Ehlathini 1980.* Radio Play. Cassette Umhlobo Wenene FM. 1980.

The Dark Edge

THE DARK EDGE of African Literature proposes arguments and theories for interpretation or exposition of Africa's modern fictions irrespective of the language of narrative. It attempts to discern how such interpretations of contemporary history may be received from an African perspective and what implications for African cultures and literatures abound by such experience. Starting with a writer's profile of twentieth century African dictatorships and the African writer, its Critical Approaches on Somali, Nigerian, Kenyan, Angolan, Sudanese Literatures present many different, if often unrecognised, materials on uprising and resistance to readers of African literature. The physical and psychological dislocation by war, the controversy about the relational quality and dependent nature of text on context, and the exigency that informs the deliberate distortions of certain figures and images by contemporary African writers are some of the significant exegesis of this volume.

.

African Library of Critical Writing

Liberian professor of African languages and literature, founder of the Society of African Folklore, and Literary Society International, LSi, Charles Smith, is editor of the Critical Writing Series on African Literature with Nigerian Chin Ce, books, news, reviews editor and research and creative writer. As one of the younger stream of poets from Africa, Ce is also the author of several works of fiction and essays on African and Caribbean literature.

African Books Network

AFRICAN Books Network with its cosmopolitan outlook is poised to meet the book needs of African generations in times to come. Since the year 2000 when we joined the highway of online solutions in publishing and distribution, our African alliance to global information development excels in spite of challenges in the region. Our select projects have given boost to the renaissance of a whole generation of dynamic literature. In our wake is the harvest of titles that have become important referrals in contemporary literary studies. With print issues followed by eContent and eBook versions, our network has demonstrated its commitment to the vision of a continent bound to a common heritage. This universal publishing outlook is further evidenced by our participation in African Literature Research projects. For everyone on deck, a hands-on interactive is the deal which continues to translate to more flexibility in line with global trends ensuring that African writers are part of the information gobalisation of the present.

   As one of Africa's mainstream book publishing and distribution networks, many authors may look to us for to privileged assistance regarding affiliate international and local publishing and distribution service

"Our select projects at African Books Network have given boost to the renaissance of a whole generation of dynamic literature."